FAMILY WALKS

IN THE DARK PEAK

Norman Taylor

Scarthin Books, Cromford, Derbyshire   1989

FAMILY WALKS
IN THE DARK PEAK

Family Walks Series
General Editor: Norman Taylor

THE COUNTRY CODE
Guard against all risk of fire
Fasten all gates
Keep dogs under proper control
Keep to paths across farm land
Avoid damaging fences, hedges and walls
Leave no litter
Safeguard water supplies
Protect wildlife, wild plants and trees
Go carefully on country roads
Respect the life of the countryside

Published 1986. Revised 1989.

Phototypesetting, printing by Higham Press Ltd., Shirland, Derbyshire

ISBN 0 907758 16 9

WINDGATHER ROCKS   Route 13

Preface

One evening about four years ago, I asked Sue, my wife, for her opinion on my plan to write a family walks guide to the Peak District. She was as keen as I on the idea. What neither of us realized then was how much time and energy it would cost us both. For me, it meant hours working at the books in the attic, but it also meant that a large part of my share of the domestic responsibilities were off-loaded on to Sue. In other words, her contribution to this book and the White Peak guide was at least equal to my own, and I am deeply indebted to her for this. Others have helped in one way or another. I must thank Dave Drew, Gez Boothby and Malcolm Wharton, my critical companions on several forays. Thanks are also due to Anna Colvin and Martin Stone and their children, Martha, Madeleine and Isaac, for getting lost on a couple of walks, thereby highlighting deficiencies. Pat Parkin and Patricia Bater succeeded in finding similar ambiguities, and this with school children in tow! I must thank once again Ken Wrigley and his family, who persuaded members of Parnassus Mountaineering Club to reconnoitre possibilities. I am sure there were others I have neglected to mention, and I thank them also for their contributions, however small.

My only hope is that this combined effort has the desired effect; to make it possible for others to explore and enjoy that gem of the Midlands, the Peak District National Park.

N.T.

CROSSBILL   Reddish brown (M) Green (F) 16cm.

CONTENTS

MAP OF THE AREA

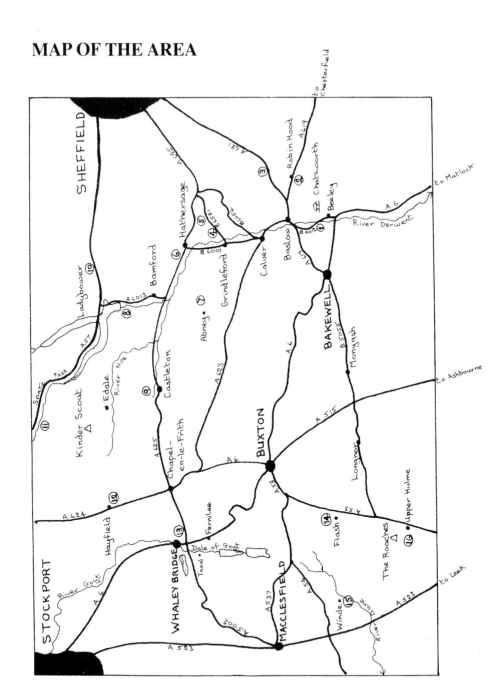

INTRODUCTION

This guide is the companion to 'Family Walks in the White Peak', all the walks being in the surrounding hills, moors and valleys that comprise the Dark Peak. As with the White Peak guide, the routes are both circular and short, varying in length from 3 miles to 6½ miles, and suited to the interests and stamina of children. They are not exclusive to families, however, and many other walkers may find this book well suited to their taste. The more strenuous sections tend, on the whole, to come early in the walk with easier, often downhill walking to complete the journey. Where possible, the walks also happen on a wayside inn or teashop roughly midway to two thirds of the way along the route. Roadwalking is kept to a minimum, and most walks avoid this altogether. In addition to stops for refreshment, all the walks have several other focal points which are attractive to children and indeed anyone with a passion for the outdoors, such as streams, woods, rocks, curiosities, scenic viewpoints, interesting wildlife and good picnic spots.

Just as the White Peak takes its name from the grey-white limestone rocks of the central area it covers, the surrounding mass of the Dark Peak similarly takes its name from its darker coloured gritstone rocks. Many people may have the impression that the Dark Peak is mostly high and bleak moorland, but this is not the case. Whilst the area to the north of the White Peak, which includes Kinder Scout and Bleaklow, does exhibit these characteristics, its rocky stream-filled guillies, its pine forests and man-made lakes provide much scenic contrast. And to either side of the White Peak is a land of 'edges' and ridges, rivers and natural woodland, low lying pastures and ancient settlements. In other words, the Dark Peak has a great deal to offer to those who are prepared to explore it the only proper way - on foot.

Choosing a walk

Unless the children taking part are seasoned walkers, it is best not to be too ambitious at first; walking along uneven footpaths or scaling a hillside is hard going if you are not used to it. In the case of very young children, start by walking interesting parts of the lower level routes, and even then be prepared to turn back; the object of the exercise is to introduce them to the joys of the countryside and not to put them off walking forever! When a full walk is planned, it is a good idea to make contingency plans so that if the party gets halfway along a route and the youngsters are on the point of rebellion, rescue can be arranged by meeting motorised friends at the pub en route, or by one of the party hurrying back to collect the transport.

Whilst for one reason or another some of the walks in this guide are only suitable for older children, by using this in combination with the White Peak guide a sufficient number of short and easy walks should be found to keep a family with young children well occupied for many a weekend outing.

To assist with the choosing of routes, they are listed according to difficulty at the back of the book.

Allowing sufficient time

Each walk is intended as the best part of a day's outing, allowing time for play, exploration and rest stops. It is better to over-estimate rather than under-estimate the time it may take, and then have to 'route march' the latter part of the journey. As a rough guide, allow a pace of around a mile per hour for the younger child, graduating to two miles per hour for the seasoned eleven year old. Where a hill climb is involved, add on extra time dependent on the size and fitness of the children in the party.

What to wear

British weather being what it is, it is best to go prepared for the worst, and even on a dry day there is always the chance that a youngster will end up soaked if the walk follows a stream or uses stepping stones. For the grown-ups, traditional hiking boots are best in the sort of terrain encountered in the Dark Peak. Children quickly grow out of expensive walking boots but other kinds of less expensive sturdy and waterproof footwear are available which act as a good substitute. Waterproof outer clothes are essential for every member of the party - never rely on it not to rain! A spare sweater for the youngsters is advisable, and a complete change of clothing is a must for the more accident-prone little ones. If the walks are being attempted in the colder months, make sure that the children are very well insulated to being with - a child loses body heat more rapidly than the average healthy adult.

The weather

In the Peak District, both during and after prolonged wet spells footpaths can become extremely muddy and slippery, and stepping stones can be impassable. This should be considered when planning expeditions. On the other hand, if you wait for the skies to clear, many opportunities will be missed. Just make sure the party is well insulated, and be prepared to lower your sights for the day.

Those venturing on to the higher moors and exposed hills and ridges should remember that the weather can change rapidly, and that even in midsummer cold winds and lashing rain can make it feel like winter at higher altitudes. So check the weather forecast for the region and go adequately prepared.

Footpaths

Apart from the two walks through Chatsworth, which use certain private footpaths open to the public in the summer season, all the walks in this guide follow public rights of way or concessionary footpaths. Where concessionary footpaths are used, this is clearly indicated on the maps provided. In the unlikely event of these being closed to the public, either temporarily or permanently, I have indicated, where possible, alternative routes using public footpaths.

In most cases, paths are well worn and easy to follow, although there are a few exceptions where, because of infrequent use, the route is not evident. However, the routes are described in sufficient detail for this not to pose problems in route finding. From time to time, farmers have been known to block off a stile on a public right of way. In the unlikely event of this happening, use your initiative but avoid damage to fences and walls.

The maps

With the exception of Route 11, the maps in this guide in combination with the route descriptions are sufficiently detailed to be used without reference to any other maps of the area. Nevertheless, many walkers will wish to take the standard Ordnance Survey sheets with them, and appropriate grid references are given with each route.

Refreshments

Most of the pubs en route allow children accompanied by adults into their premises. Many also have beer gardens, whilst at others walls or grassed areas serve the same purpose. In the few cases where children are not allowed inside, the pubs are mentioned nevertheless, since their locations are sufficiently pleasant to drink and relax outside if the weather is good.

I would advise those planning a pub lunch to aim to arrive at the desired pub before 1.30 p.m. since catering often ceases well before closing time.

Teashop opening times vary according to the time of year and expected custom, but most can be relied upon to open until five or six o'clock during the summer season.

Transport to the area

Although I have assumed that most people will travel to the area by car, a fair number of the starts of walks can be reached by bus. In some others it is possible to start and finish at another point along the route, where there is a bus stop. Brief details are given at the end of the route descriptions, and there is a list of bus operators at the back of the book.

Symbols used on the route maps

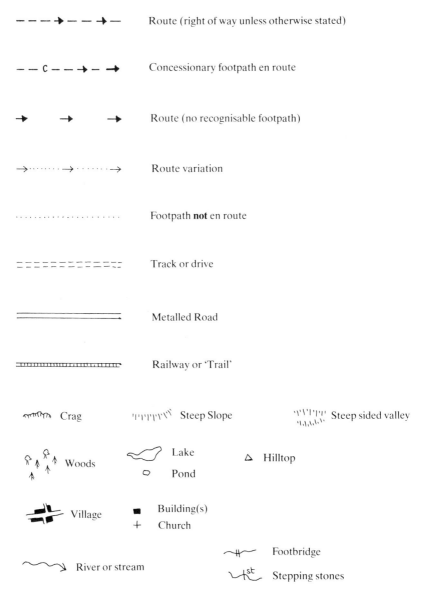

– – – ➜ – – ➜ –   Route (right of way unless otherwise stated)

– – c – – ➜ – ➜   Concessionary footpath en route

➜   ➜   ➜   Route (no recognisable footpath)

→ ⋯⋯ → ⋯⋯ →   Route variation

⋯⋯⋯⋯⋯⋯⋯⋯   Footpath **not** en route

= = = = = = = = = = = = =   Track or drive

━━━━━━━━━━   Metalled Road

▭▭▭▭▭▭▭▭▭▭▭   Railway or 'Trail'

ᴧᴧᴧᴧ Crag   ꞌꞌꞌꞌꞌꞌꞌ Steep Slope   ꞌꞌꞌꞌꞌꞌ Steep sided valley

🌲🌲🌲 Woods   Lake   △ Hilltop

     ○ Pond

Village   ■ Building(s)

     + Church

River or stream   Footbridge

     Stepping stones

④ etc. Number corresponds with route description

8

South Chatsworth and Beeley

Outline   Calton Lees ~ Chatsworth House ~ Stand Wood ~ Beeley ~ Calton Lees.

Summary   A varied walk combining riverside, forest, lake and open moorland as well as a visit to a typical Derbyshire village with a friendly inn. Good footpaths are followed with the uphill part concentrated in a short section immediately behind Chatsworth House. All the major features in the Chatsworth woods are encountered to produce a first rate walk with lots of interest for all concerned. The section between Chatsworth House and the Hunting Tower is over private tracks and paths which may not be open during the winter months. Many of the other paths are Concessionary Paths and details of closures are advertised in the local press.

Attractions   The walk begins on the banks of the River Derwent, the section near the car park being a very popular spot with tourists out for an afternoon stroll. Along the quieter stretches, mallard and dipper are the more regular inhabitants. Though less frequently seen, heron are also common along the Derwent.

Once across the bridge, the first curiosity is Queen Mary's Bower, a strange structure worth investigating. A little further on is the home of the Devonshires, the most palatial building in this part of England. The original house was built by Bess of Hardwick and her second husband, William Cavendish, in 1552. It was here that Mary Queen of Scots was imprisoned on five occasions. The present mansion was begun in 1687 for the fourth Earl of Devonshire, who became the first Duke for his part in securing the throne for William of Orange.

The park was landscaped by Capability Brown in the 18th century, whilst the gardens, lakes and water features were the creation of Joseph Paxton in the 19th century. It was the latter who 'moved' the village of Edensor to a new site "where it did not mar the Duke's view". Stand Wood, situated behind the house, is as much a man-made creation as the gardens below, for until the 18th century this slope was a bare and bleak hillside with a few ancient oaks and yews, some of which still stand. The rich and varied wood that exists today is the result of planting, protection from grazing animals, cropping for timber and natural regeneration.

continued on page 12

9

Route 1

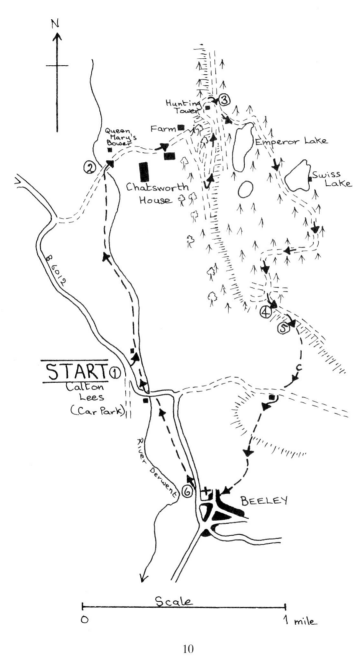

Route 1

South Chatsworth and Beeley

5½ miles

START *At Calton Lees car park/picnic area on the B.6012 a mile south of Chatsworth House. (G.R. 258685)*

ROUTE

1. *On leaving the car park, cross the main road and go down to the river to follow it upstream to a bridge.*

2. *Cross the bridge and continue up to and past Chatsworth Farmyard, following the tarmac drive uphill into Stand Wood. Turn sharp left at the first tarmac track on the left. Follow this up past the broken aqueduct to the Hunting Tower. Alternatively, leave the track a few metres beyond the right-angled bend on the top side of the Farmyard and take an ascending footpath, then steps to the same point.*

3. *Follow the track around the Tower or pass to the right of the Tower and regain the track. Continue along this track, taking a left fork, and on past Emperor and Swiss Lakes. The track eventually bends to the right, then to the left, before reaching a crossroads. Go straight across, and walk on for about another 100 metres as far as a gate and stile on the left (yellow arrow).*

4. *Follow the yellow arrow and continue along a rough track for a short distance only to another yellow arrow marking on the right.*

5. *Bear right down the footpath and follow this to another track. Cross it and continue past farm buildings and through a gate. Keep to the wall on the left as far as a stile. Continue down through fields with stiles to Beeley, using the church tower as a marker.*

6. *On the opposite side of the main road to St. Anne's Church is a handgate. Pass through and follow the footpath upstream to the bridge at Calton Lees. Cross the bridge, then leave the road again to continue along the left bank of the river before going up to the car park.*

ACCESS BY BUS

To Chatsworth House and Beeley from Sheffield and Ilkeston summer Sundays (South Yorkshire/Trent), also summer Sundays and Bank Holidays (East Midland/Crosville), and Monday to Friday (Silver Service) from Chesterfield, Macclesfield and Matlock.

Chatsworth Farmyard is passed on the way up to the woods. The farm exhibits, which include horses, pigs, poultry, cattle, sheep, a fish farm and items connected with forestry, make a visit very worthwhile, especially when the best adventure playground in these parts is thrown in with the price. And this is why a visit should perhaps be postponed for another occasion!

In the wood, the waterfall at the aqueduct provides a good excuse to stop and explore, and right at the top of the hill is the Hunting Tower with its iron cannon. The cannon came from a ship that fought at Trafalgar. The tower was built around 1582 as a summer house for Bess of Hardwick.

Further on are the Emperor and Swiss Lakes. These provide an ideal habitat for several species of wildfowl. Tufted duck, sandpiper and moorhen are often seen here, whilst great-crested and little grebe, shoveller and teal may occasionally be sighted. For the hawk enthusiasts, buzzard and sparrowhawk are said to nest hereabouts. Of the mammals that might be seen, look out for grey squirrels and, on the lakes, the water vole. In the more open spaces alongside the track, turn your gaze to the wild flowers, which include wood anemone, dog's mercury, wood sorrel and harebell.

Down from the moor is Beeley, an attractive little village with quaint 17th century cottages and an equally quaint 17th century inn. Its church dates from the 13th century, although various bits and pieces have been added since. The 15th century battlemented tower underlines the church's other former purpose as a stronghold. In connection with this, an old yew by the porch is said to be as old as the oldest part of the church, and the yew provided the raw material for that lethal weapon of bygone days, the longbow.

Refreshments Chatsworth. Tea shop.

Devonshire Arms at Beeley. Children admitted, snacks available.

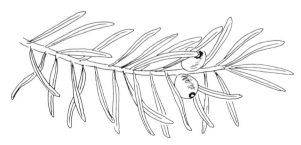

YEW Berries poisonous

Route 2 4½ miles

North Chatsworth

Outline   Robin Hood ~ Stand Wood ~ Chatsworth House ~ Robin Hood.

Summary   This walk complements the preceding one and is just as delightful an excursion with a lot of interest. The first part follows a track below Chatsworth Edge, after which a short, stiff ascent is made to the top of the quarried Dobb Edge. From here, there are fine views of the Derwent Valley and surrounding hills. Tracks are then followed through woodland, which eventually lead down to Chatsworth House and Farmyard. The return is a pleasant stroll, mostly on the level, through the deer park. The section between Chatsworth House and the Hunting Tower is over private tracks and paths which may not be open during the winter months. Many of the other paths are Concessionary Paths and details of closures are advertised in the local press.

Attractions   On leaving Robin Hood - the place, not the legendary figure - the first interesting feature encountered is Chatsworth Edge, the most southerly of the gritstone crags on an escarpment stretching twenty miles northwards to Howden Moor. This hard layer of sandstone was laid down originally as silt over 250 million years ago when the Peak District was part of a massive river delta.

Before entering Stand Wood, a quarried edge is passed. Unfinished millstones lie amidst the spoil heaps as reminders of a once thriving industry in the Peak District. Such millstones were manufactured for use both in flour mills and in grinding blades in Sheffield. Unlike limestone scars, gritstone quarries blend more easily into the natural landscape, and the scene hereabouts has a wild and unspoilt look, this enhanced by the natural oak woodland and the presence of fallow deer belonging to the estate.

Stand Wood, on the other hand, is a man-made feature that is so well planned and nurtured that it looks natural. Many different species can be seen. The main varieties of softwood tend to be Norway Spruce, Larch and Scots Pine, still used for mining-timber and fence-posts. The spruce, our traditional Christmas tree, is also extensively planted for pulpwood and has been cultivated in England for 300 years or so. The indigenous trees are the oak and the yew, of which one or two ancient specimens still exist, whilst the Spanish chestnut, beech, sycamore and various other species were planted between 1750 and 1850.

continued on page 16

13

Route 2

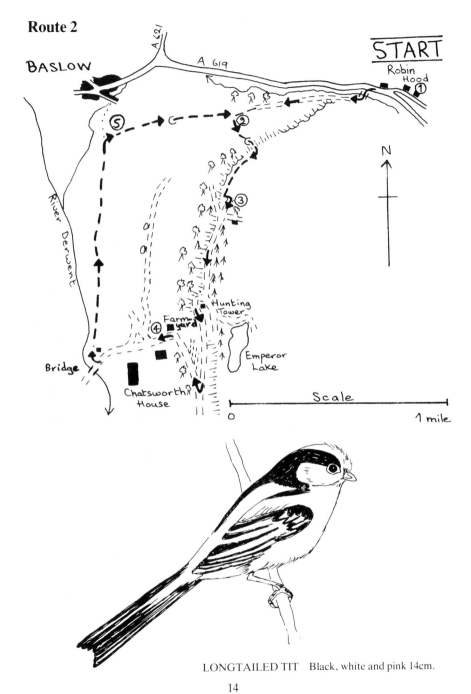

LONGTAILED TIT   Black, white and pink 14cm.

14

Route 2   North Chatsworth   4½ miles

START   *At Birchen Edge car park adjacent to the Robin Hood Inn on the A.619 about 2 miles east of Baslow. (G.R. 282722)*

ROUTE

1. *From the car park, go the the main road and turn right. On the opposite side of the road in 150 metres is a wooden stile by a footpath sign. Cross this and descend steps to a footbridge. Continue over this and bear right to join a track. Follow this along the foot of Chatsworth Edge to a gate and high stone stile. Cross it and a field to another stone stile. You are now entering Chatsworth Park.*

2. *After crossing this stile, follow the wall up to the left. Continue all the way up to the top, then go right above the disused quarry. A stone stepping stile is soon reached at the edge of a plantation. Cross this and go left by the wall to join a track.*

3. *Turn right here, and continue along the track for ½ mile to a T-junction on the far side of which, and concealed by trees, is the Hunting Tower. Turn right at the T-junction and follow the track (Holmes Lane) downhill to another junction, passing the broken aqueduct on the way. Turn sharp right and continue downhill to Chatsworth Farmyard. Alternatively, leave the track immediately below the Hunting Tower to descend more steeply and directly to the same point.*

4. *Continue down past the Farmyard and, keeping Chatsworth House to your left, make for the river at Chatsworth Bridge. On reaching the Bridge turn right through the handgate - still on the south side of the river - and walk behind the strange looking structure known as Queen Mary's Bower along a track towards the Cricket Ground. Carry on straight ahead, ignoring tracks right and left, to a kissing gate at the northern entrance to the Park.*

5. *Turn right here and follow the signpost marked "Concessionary Footpath, Robin Hood 1½m". The path is vague at first, but after crossing a drive becomes more obvious. Continue to the second of the two high stone stepping stiles crossed earlier. Retrace your steps to finish.*

ACCESS BY BUS

To Robin Hood from Chesterfield, Bakewell and Matlock (Silver Service), daily.

To Chatsworth House and Beeley from Sheffield and Ilkeston summer Sundays (South Yorkshire/Trent), also summer Sundays and Bank Holidays (East Midland/Crosville), and Monday to Friday (Silver Service) from Chesterfield, Macclesfield and Matlock.

Needless to say, birdlife in the woods is rich and varied, and quite rare as well as common species can often be picked out with a little patience. In the deciduous woodland, keep an eye out for the long-tailed tit, an easy bird to identify because of its distinctive black, pink and white colouring. Amongst the pines, goldcrest, tree-creeper and, occasionally, crossbill may be seen.

Before descending to Chatsworth Farmyard, the Hunting Tower with its iron cannon is passed (see Route 1). Further on down the track - part of an ancient packhorse trail known as Holmes Lane - is a series of waterfalls ending in a broken aqueduct that was built in 1839. The water drops 80 feet here and on windless days it is possible to stand behind the waterfall without getting wet, unless you are a child, that is!

Chatsworth Farmyard, with its adventure playground, is a worthy stopping-off point but a difficult one to leave! Once away from the hubbub, deer, ducks, pheasant and wide open spaces provide interest on the way back.

Refreshments   Chatsworth. Tea shop.

Robin Hood Inn. Beer garden, snacks available, children admitted.

RING OUZEL
Black and white 24cm.

Route 3   **3 miles**

Birchen and Gardom's Edges

Outline A.621 (Curbar/Chesterfield crossroads) ~ Birchen Edge ~ Robin Hood ~ Gardom's Edge ~ A.621.

Summary An easy moorland walk with footpaths marking the way. Any ascent en route is gradual and the walk is, therefore, suitable for younger children. A rather boggy patch is encountered in the first quarter of a mile, though the rest of the walk presents no further wet problems. The first half of the excursion is in open country, whilst the return leg is more wooded and, in places, the footpath battles for survival amongst tall, dense bracken. This, the views and the crags make for a varied and stimulating walk.

Attractions Birchen Edge is popular with novice climbers and, on warm weekends, many of the climbs are laced with rope and tackle. To stop and watch is compulsive for young and old alike, the younger ones eager to have a go. This they can do in relative safety on The Three Ships, smaller rocks above the crag a few metres away from Nelson's Monument. As well as watching the antics of climbers, it is also fun listening to their dialogue as problems are encountered.

Nelson's Monument, erected in 1805, commemorates Nelson's victory at Trafalgar. Across the valley is a similar monument commemorating another fighting hero, the Duke of Wellington.

Halfway along the walk is a cluster of buildings and an inn, both going by the name of Robin Hood. In other than name, it boasts no connection with the legendary figure, although this area was at the western edge of Sherwood Forest in medieval times.

On approaching Gardom's Edge, the footpath forces its way through dense bracken. But for human traffic, it would be in danger of becoming totally overgrown during the summer. Bracken, however, is good news for children, for it provides perfect cover for stalking and surprising those bringing up the rear.

Gardom's Edge, named after John Gardom of Bubnell, who built the original Calver Mill, presents a somewhat wilder aspect than Birchen Edge.

It is also less popular with climbers because the climbs are generally harder, more forbidding and take longer to dry out. Because of this, Gardom's is a good place for bird-watching. Along the more open sections wheatear and ring ouzel may be seen, the latter being more

continued on page 20

17

Route 3

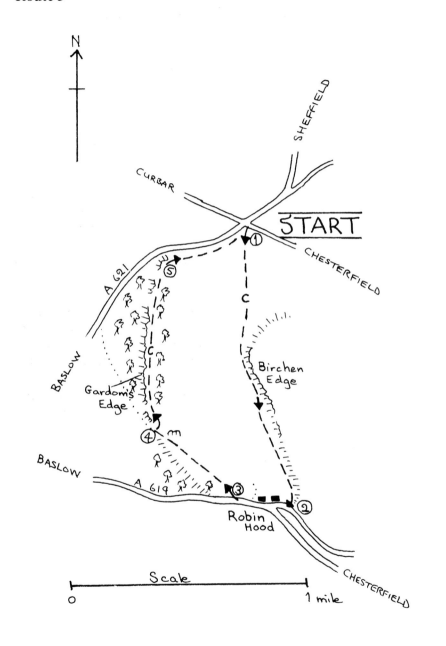

Route 3   3 miles

Birchen and Gardom's Edges

START   *On the A.621 Sheffield to Baslow road about 2 miles from Baslow, and at a crossroads signposted Curbar to the west and Chesterfield/Cutthorpe to the east. Park near the junction on the Chesterfield road adjacent to an obvious ladder stile.* (G.R. 278740)

ROUTE

1. *Cross the stile and bear left along the obvious footpath, ignoring a minor footpath forking off to the right. Continue through an often boggy section to Birchen Edge. Follow the footpath below the crag, which leads down to a minor road at Robin Hood.*

2. *Turn right and walk past the Robin Hood Inn to the junction with main road. Turn right and follow the pavement downhill for 200 metres to a stone stile on the right (not the wooden stile giving access to a campsite).*

3. *After crossing the stile, follow the gradually ascending footpath, which soon becomes a trek through bracken, for about ½ mile to an open gateway. Just before this is reached, to the right of the footpath are prominent rocks which act as a direction marker.*

4. *Leave the main footpath at this point and take a minor footpath following the wall up to the right. This soon bears left with the wall. To avoid walking through heather, keep left to follow a footpath, vague to begin with, along the top of Gardom's Edge. Continue to a wooden stile at the other side of which are rocks overlooking the A.621.*

5. *Ignore a footpath descending directly to the road. Instead, bear right at the rocks and continue along a narrow footpath back to the start.*

ACCESS BY BUS

To Robin Hood only, from Chesterfield, Bakewell and Matlock (Silver Service), daily.

difficult to spot. In the wooded area below the crags, look out for the robin-like redstart.

The wilderness below Gardon's Edge is accessible at one or two places but care should be exercised in the vicinity of these crags. Only for the agile, scrambling about amongst the overgrown quarry debris at the foot of the cliffs can be quite an adventure. To escape from here, continue along to the end of the main part of the crag and an easy ascent back to the footpath. Should the younger element be intent on climbing something, at the far end of the crag, overlooking the road and by the side of the footpath, small boulders provide scope for this in safer surroundings. Even here, however, adults should keep a wary eye.

Refreshments Robin Hood Inn, Robin Hood. Children admitted, beer garden, snacks available.

THE PINNACLE, FROGGATT EDGE

20

Froggatt Edge and Derwent Valley

Outline Haywood Picnic Area ~ Froggatt Edge ~ Froggatt ~ Grindleford ~ Haywood Picnic Area.

Summary A fine walk that would start at Grindleford if the village had a car park. As it is, the most strenuous part of the walk is the last half mile up the steep wooded slope between the village and Haywood Picnic Area. The rest of the walk is either on the level or downhill. From the Picnic Area a track is followed along the top of Froggatt Edge, a popular place for a Sunday saunter because of the excellent views of the Derwent Valley and surrounding moors. Unless the longer variation is taken, the track is left for a footpath leading down from the crags to the village of Froggatt and the River Derwent. Another footpath links Froggatt with Grindleford, passing through attractive woodland on the way.

Attractions About ¾ mile along the Froggatt Edge track, immediately to the left is a small stone circle. Along with other similar ones in the Peak District, these are now thought to be the remains of Bronze Age burial mounds, or barrows, the stone still standing representing the inner lining of such tombs.

A little further on, weathered 'boulders' of gritstone which are flat underneath provide scope for climbing. On the same subject, Froggatt Edge is one of the classic rock-climbing 'edges' and certainly one of the busiest. Adjacent to where the footpath doubles back downhill from the foot of the crags is a classic, hard Joe Brown route, the Great Slab. Should you be lucky, you may see one of today's young 'tigers' scaling the climb. A route up the nose of the Pinnacle, 50 metres further on, is another of Brown's famous firsts. Nowadays, climbing standards are such that these routes no longer represent the top grade, although many would-be conquerors retreat on reaching the hardest moves.

Froggatt, with its 17th century bridge, is a quaint old village that may once have housed some of the quarrymen who worked the Edge for building stone and for millstones. Beyond here is Froggatt Wood, a wild place with a somewhat mystical air. Less mystical is a long, rope swing across a stream in the wood that belongs to local children. This is only recommended for lightweights!

continued on page 24

21

Route 4

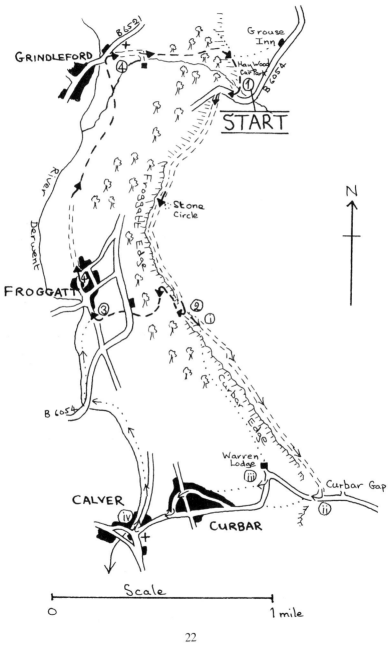

Route 4

4 miles

(Variation 6 miles)

Froggatt Edge and Derwent Valley

START *The route is described from the Haywood National Trust car park and picnic area ¼ mile south of the Grouse Inn on the B.6054 and 2½ miles north of Calver. (G.R. 256777)*

ROUTE

1. *Cross the stream on the south side of the car park to reach the main road. Turn right, then go across to a white gate and the start of a track. Continue along this for just over a mile to prominent boulders above the highest part of Froggatt Edge crag. About 200 metres beyond these is a natural break in the crag.*

2. *Turn right off the track at this point and scramble down to a footpath that doubles back immediately below the rocks. Follow this to within 50 metres of a prominent 60 foot high pinnacle and look carefully for a footpath that doubles back downhill to the left. Follow this down into woods, over a ladder stile, and on down to a main road. The Chequers Inn is immediately to the right. Cross the road to a stile opposite, and continue descending to a minor road.*

3. *Turn right into Froggatt. Stay on this road until it bends uphill to the right. Leave the road and carry straight on in front of a row of houses. The road soon becomes a track, then a footpath, leading through Froggatt Wood and eventually joining the main road in Grindleford on the Sheffield side of the bridge.*

4. *Turn right and walk along the pavement to a track on the right in 50 metres. This is adjacent to a church and opposite a garage. Follow the track up to where it bends right. Leave the track more or less on the bend, and continue straight on over a stile and along a footpath on the left of a stream. Follow this up through the woods to a junction with another footpath near the top. Turn right to finish back at the car park.*

LONGER VARIATION

As for 1 above but:

i   *Instead of turning off the track at Froggatt Edge, continue along it for another mile, where it joins the minor road at Curbar Gap.*

ii *Turn right and follow the road down for ¼ mile to a stile on the right 100 metres past Warren Lodge, which itself is on a sharp bend.*

If the longer variation is taken, the even more impressive main buttress of Cubar Edge is passed, where onlookers can amuse themselves watching climbers grapple with the steep and difficult rock, chalk bags at the ready to give fingers better adhesion on small or rounded holds.

On the way back, Calver Mill can be seen across the river. Now manufacturing stainless steel sinks, it was originally a spinning mill built in 1786 and operated by water power. From here, the walk follows the riverside to Froggatt. On hot days, it is sorely tempting to strip off and jump into the river but this is an angler's preserve, as the many notices indicate. If you keep your eyes on the river as you walk along, you may see the odd water vole out on a forage. Other inhabitants include the grey and yellow wagtails, heron, dipper and various waterfowl.

Soon after leaving Grindleford, natural oak and birch woodland up a steep slope acts as an effective camouflage in hiding the extent of the climb from the valley. And when legs are beginning to tire, a breath can be taken to pick out some of the birdlife inhabiting the woods, which includes redstart, wood warbler and redpoll.

Refreshments   Grindleford Cafe.

Sir William at Grindleford. Children admitted, beer garden, snacks available.

Grouse Inn. Children admitted, snacks available, primitive outside seating.

Cafe at Calver Mill.

Bridge Inn at Calver Mill.

---

iii *Cross this stile and follow the footpath to a ladder stile on the right. Cross the older stile adjacent to it and continue down past a playground to a road in Curbar village. Turn right and follow the road to a crossroads. Go straight across and continue to a junction. Turn right, and walk down the road to the Bridge Inn.*

iv *Turn sharp right along the road signposted Froggatt. Follow this for ¼ mile to a stile on the left. Cross it and continue on the riverside footpath to a main road. Cross the road to pick up the continuation of the riverside footpath, which joins the road near the bridge in Froggatt. Continue as for 3 and 4 above.*

ACCESS BY BUS

To Grindleford from Ilkeston, Bakewell and Castleton (Trent), summer Sundays and Bank Holidays.

Route 5

Padley Gorge and Longshaw

Outline   Grindleford Station (Padley) ~ Padley Gorge ~ Over Owler Tor ~ Carl Wark ~ Longshaw Estate ~ Padley.

Summary   The walks are described from Padley, although other access points and car parks are marked on the accompanying map. The walking is full of interest offering a contrast between wooded gorge and open moorland with several good viewpoints en route. If the longer route is taken, an ascending footpath along Padley Gorge is followed, after which a small section of moorland near a main road is climbed to a point overlooking the Hope Valley. From here, the walk continues to the hillfort of Carl Wark, passing through a short, boggy section just below it. This is the highest point reached, and the rest is on the level or downhill. The next objective is Longshaw Estate, an area of partially tamed moorland with both open and wooded landscape. After crossing Longshaw, a steep descent is made to Padley. Since some of the footpaths are of the rough and ready kind, this should be considered when selecting from the variations given.

Attractions   Padley Gorge and its woods are a natural playground for youngsters, and a summer's day can easily be spent just exploring, examining the various forms of wildlife or paddling and playing in the tumbling brook. The oak and birch woodland remains much as it was in medieval times, when it formed the north western extremity of Sherwood Forest. As with other wooded gritstone valleys, birdlife is varied, and, with patience and a bit of luck, woodpeckers, wood warbler and redstart may be observed. By the stream, grey wagtail and dipper can usually be picked out in the summer months.

The little stretch of moor to the west of the brook is another natural adventure playground and is used as such because of its accessibility from the main road. It has an abandoned quarry with rows of finished or partly worked millstones. There are nooks and crannies everywhere to investigate and weathered gritstone boulders of all shapes and sizes to climb. One of these, known as Mother Cap, is a block twenty feet in height. Such isolated stumps are the result of erosion by wind-blown loose grit - a natural form of sand-blasting, in other words.

Another interesting feature a little way across the moor is the fort at Carl Wark. Although popular belief has it that the fort dates from the

continued on page 28

25

Route 5

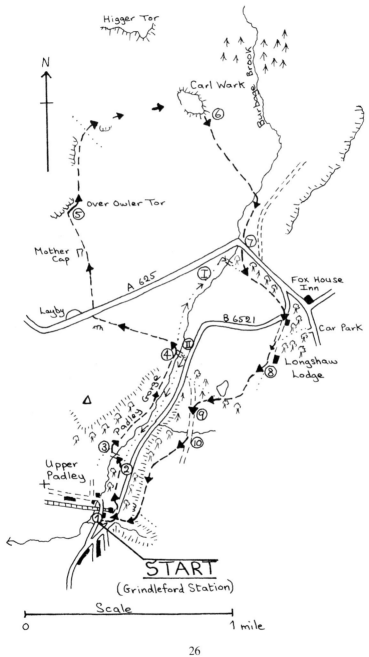

Higger Tor

N

Carl Wark

Burbage Brook

⑥

Over Owler Tor

⑤

Mother Cap

A 625

Layby

⑦

Fox House Inn

Car Park

①

B 6521

Longshaw Lodge

④ Ⅱ

⑧

Padley Gorge

△

⑨

⑩

③

②

Upper Padley

START

(Grindleford Station)

Scale

0   1 mile

Route 5

Padley Gorge and Longshaw

5½ miles

(Shorter variations 3½ and 2 miles)

START   *At Grindleford Station, about 1 mile north of Grindleford on the B.6521. (G.R. 252788).*

ROUTE

1. *To the right of the station cafe a footpath leads up to the main road. Follow this, turn left at the road, then left again at a handgate by a bus stop. Continue along a footpath as far as a second gate.*

2. *After a few metres, bear left along a path leading down to the stream and a footbridge. Continue over this and up steps on the other side to join a footpath at the top of the steep bank.*

3. *Turn right to follow the well-used footpath up through the woods to more open ground above the gorge. Stop at the next footbridge.*

4. *Go left at this point to enter a dug-out channel which leads up to the main Sheffield to Castleton road (A.625). Cross the road and a stile opposite and continue in the same direction up on to the moor ahead. A prominent tall block of gritstone, Mother Cap, comes into view. Continue towards and past this to the next rocky tor, (Over Owler Tor.)*

5. *Turn right at this point and follow a vague footpath along an edge to a sheep enclosure. Bear right here and cross boggy ground to reach Carl Wark fort.*

6. *From the fort, several alternatives present themselves, the objective being Toad's Mouth, where Burbage Brook passes beneath the A.625 at a bridge. Either take the footpath that goes down to the stream and continue along the left bank of the brook, or follow the path that stays on the right of the stream.*

7. *Cross the road and pass through a handgate on the Sheffield side of the bridge. Follow the footpath up to the left to the Grindleford road (B.6521). Cross the road to the gate house at the entrance to Longshaw Lodge, and walk along the avenue, then a footpath in front of the Lodge. Continue through a handgate.*

8. *Take the right fork here and walk down to the pond. A few metres after reaching this, bear left along a vague footpath by a copse of pine trees. Follow it to where it meets a more obvious track.*

9. *Turn left and continue along the track as far as a bridge over a stream.*

10. *A few metres beyond this, bear right off the track by two wooden posts to continue along a footpath. After passing through a handgate, the path begins to descend. Ignoring a left fork to a ladder stile, continue down more steeply through trees to the main road and the station.*

Iron Age, the structure of its walls, its position below Higgar Tor and other evidence suggest its origin is much more recent. Informed opinion dates it between 400 and 500 A.D., although its purpose still remains a mystery. After the archaeological tour, head for the huge boulders below its south wall. Stacked haphazardly against each other, these provide an ideal opportunity for 'weaselling', a game of follow-my-leader through the crevices and holes.

Longshaw Estate, famous for its annual sheepdog trials, now belongs to the National Trust. The Lodge was formerly a shooting box of the Dukes of Rutland. Somewhat resembling wild parkland, walking through the estate provides a pleasant contrast to what has gone before. The place is also famous for its variety of edible mushrooms but unless someone in the party can tell the difference between these and the poisonous varieties, picking them is not to be recommended.

If time permits at the end of the journey and sufficient enthusiasm can be rekindled after refreshments in the cafe at Grindleford Station, it is worth walking the short distance to see Padley Chapel. It is on record that Robert Eyre came home from Agincourt in 1415, married Joan Padley, and built a manor house here. The Chapel, used as a cowshed for a number of years before being restored, is now all that remains of Padley Hall.

Refreshments   Cafe, Grindleford Station. Licenced.
Fox House Inn. Outside seating, snacks available.
Cafe, Longshaw Estate.

SHORTER VARIATIONS As for 1 to 3 above, then:

I *Continue along the footpath on the left bank of the stream to a third footbridge. Cross it and follow the ascending footpath. Continue as for 7 to 10 above. (3½ miles)*

or II *Cross the second footbridge, turn right and walk back along the opposite side of the gorge. (2 miles).*

ACCESS BY BUS

To Fox House/Longshaw from Chesterfield and Hayfield (Ringwood), summer Sundays and Bank Holidays; from Buxton and Sheffield (Trent), daily; from Sheffield (South Yorkshire), daily.

To Maynard Arms Hotel (Grindleford Station) from Sheffield (South Yorkshire), daily.

BRITISH RAIL from Sheffield and Manchester to Grindleford.

FAIR BROOK, KINDER Route 11

29

LITTLE JOHN'S
GRAVE
HATHERSAGE
Route 6

ABNEY   Route 7

Route 6 6 miles

Offerton Moor and Highlow Brook

Outline   Hathersage ~ Offerton Hall ~ Offerton Moor ~ Stoke Ford ~ Leadmill ~ Hathersage.

Summary   A walk full of contrast, it starts in low lying meadowland, climbs to the top of a moor, then descends to a wooded valley to complete the circuit. On leaving Hathersage, the River Derwent is crossed on stepping stones, after which a mile of strenuous uphill walking leads to the lofty heights of Offerton Moor. The effort is rewarded with splendid views of the area. From here, the rest is more or less downhill. The moor is quitted for a particularly attractive wooded vale, whose stream is followed down to where it meets the Derwent at the hamlet of Leadmill. The final leg is a short stroll through riverside meadows back to Hathersage.

Attractions   Soon out of Hathersage, the footpath follows the river bank for a short distance. Keep an eye out for heron over this stretch. The stepping stones, crossing as they do a fully fledged river, are an immediate attraction for youngsters. Whilst these usually present no problems during the summer season, after heavy rain they can be completely covered, when an attempted crossing would be foolhardy. Recent weather should therefore be considered before setting out, to avoid disappointment.

    After a prolonged ascent from the river, 16th century Offerton Hall, now a farm, provides an excuse to stop, rest and ponder over its past. As with Hazelford Hall, which is passed on the way back, and Highlow Hall above Highlow Brook, it was owned by the Eyre family. It is reputed that the original Eyre was given the name, along with land in these parts, by William the Conqueror. The person in question was supposed to have saved William from suffocating by prising off the latter's helmet, which had been crushed against his face at the Battle of Hastings. Hence the name 'eyre', which means air. A fuller account of this tale is displayed on the wall at the Eyre Arms at Hassop.

    On leaving the Hall, a short, steep ascent leads finally to the top of the moor. From this high vantage point, on a clear day, many features of the Derwent Valley and the eastern moors can be made out. And it is only from Offerton Moor that the dam which holds back Ladybower can be seen end on. Looking north-eastwards with a powerful pair of binoculars, it might even be possible to make out the climbers on Stanage Edge.

continued on page 34

Route 6

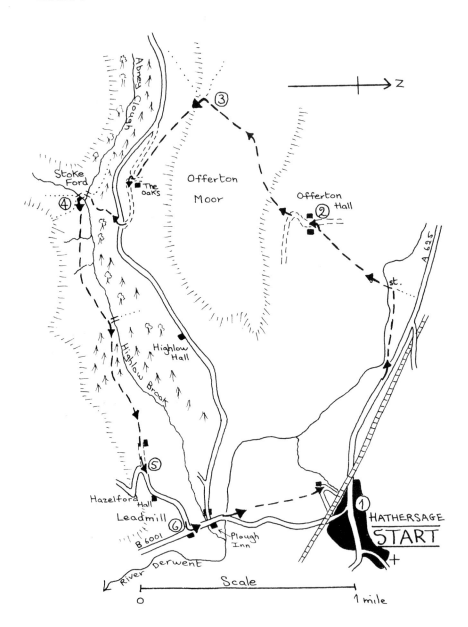

Abney Clough

Stoke Ford

④

The Oaks

③

Offerton Moor

Offerton Hall

②

st.

A 625

Highlow Brook

Highlow Hall

⑤

Hazelford Hall

Leadmill

⑥

B 6001

Plough Inn

River Derwent

① HATHERSAGE **START**

Scale

0   1 mile

Route 6   6 miles

Offerton Moor and Highlow Brook

START   *At Hathersage.*

ROUTE

1. *Walk out of Hathersage in the direction of Castleton. Continue under and beyond the railway bridge to a stile by a gate on the left and opposite a large road sign. Continue through the stile and bear right. The footpath comes down to the River Derwent. Continue upstream to stepping stones. Cross these, then follow the path signposted Offerton. After a steep climb, the footpath reaches a track by Offerton Hall Farm.*

2. *Turn left and continue up the track, passing the farm gateway, to a sharp left-hand bend. Leave the track here and cross the leftmost of two stiles. Go up steeply for a short distance, then bear right along the now more obvious footpath. Carry on up to the top of the hill and on across the moor. Shortly after the footpath begins to descend the other side, it is crossed by another footpath.*

3. *Turn left here and follow the rough footpath through bracken for ½ mile to a cottage (The Oaks). Go down to a gate and gravel track immediately on the right of the cottage. Follow the track down to a minor road. Cross it and the stile opposite (signposted Stoke Ford), then bear right down a field to another stile. Continue down to Stoke Ford. Cross two footbridges.*

4. *Bear left immediately to follow a gradually ascending footpath. This runs more or less parallel to the stream below. At one point, the path crosses a gully and climbs higher before descending to the stream at a footbridge. Do not cross the footbridge. Instead, cross a stile to the right of it, then continue through a larch plantation. The footpath soon joins a track by an old cottage. Continue along the track to a minor road.*

5. *Turn left and follow the road to a T-junction.*

6. *Turn left again. The Plough Inn is on the right in 150 metres. Continue past the Inn and over the bridge to a stile on the left. Follow the footpath through fields to a minor road near the railway viaduct at Hathersage. Turn left to finish by the Little John.*

ACCESS BY BUS

To Hathersage from Sheffield and Castleton (South Yorkshire/Trent), daily.

British Rail from Sheffield and Manchester.

After crossing the top of the heather moor, there is a fine view of the moors to the south and the deeply cut valley of Abney Clough.

After the moorland trek, a descent through a jungle of bracken follows, with all the delights this has to offer the young and the young at heart.

Once down into Abney Clough, the landscape changes abruptly. The little valley, etched out by the stream over thousands of years, is clothed in woodland, some natural, some man-made. Usually a quiet place - except on the odd occasions that a coach-load of ramblers descends on it like an army of ants - it is worth investigating the birdlife. The deciduous woodland is the habitat of both the green and greater spotted woodpecker, though they are more often heard than seen. In the pine woods, crossbill may be seen from time to time. Slightly larger than a sparrow, and rather parrotlike in appearance, the crossbill rarely comes to ground and is most likely to be seen feeding on pine cones.

A short stroll from Leadmill leads back into Hathersage, which if time permits, is worth exploring. As early as the 16th century the village had an iron-working industry. In the 19th century, it employed people in both millstone making and wiredrawing for needles and umbrella frames. Charlotte Bronte stayed at the vicarage, and her wanderings near to Hathersage gave her the material for her novel, "Jane Eyre". The church to which the vicarage belongs dates from the 14th century but the major attraction for visitors is Little John's grave in the churchyard. Tradition has it that a certain giant of a man called John Little was a nailmaker in the village in the 13th century. At that time, Hathersage was on the northwest fringe of a much larger Sherwood Forest. There is also some foundation of truth in the existence of a Robin Hood character, a rebel Saxon lord "holding out against the Norman invaders" in this then remote area roundabout the time John lived. The rest is left to conjecture.

Refreshments

Plough Inn at Leadmill. Children admitted, snacks available.

Hathersage Inn, Hathersage. Children admitted, snacks available, no muddy boots.

George Inn, Hathersage. Children admitted, snacks available.

Scotchman's Pack. Children admitted, beer garden, snacks available.

Little John. Children admitted, beer garden, snacks available.

(Shorter variation 3 miles)

Abney Clough and Bretton

Outline   Abney ~ Stoke Ford ~ Bretton Clough ~ Nether Bretton ~ Bretton ~ Abney.

Summary   The walk traces a route along two quiet and secluded little valleys with the option of calling in at an old inn from which there is one of the best views in the Peak District. With streams, footbridges, woods and good picnic spots, it is particularly attractive to children. From the remote hamlet of Abney, a footpath down Abney Clough is followed to its junction with Bretton Clough. A gradual ascent is then made along the latter to a gully from where a short, steep climb leads up to Nether Bretton and the track into Bretton. The shorter walk omits this steeper section. Whichever route is taken, a descent to a footbridge over Bretton Brook is the next objective. From here, the footpath climbs again for a short distance before descending to Abney.

Attractions   Abney is a delightful little hamlet composed mainly of small farms devoted to livestock. On higher land nearby is Abney Grange, once a monastic sheepfarm owned by Welbeck Abbey. Abney Clough - 'clough' meaning valley - starts just to the west of the hamlet, where it is little more than a deeply cut gully. But over a very short distance it attains the proportions of a steep sided valley. With more natural woodland fringing the stream, and larch plantation covering the steeper slopes, Abney Clough is an altogether pleasant place to be. For those with an eye for the plant life, the valley supports an uncommon variety of ferns.

Where Bretton Clough meets Abney Clough is Stoke Ford. The ford no longer exists, and a wooden footbridge marks the spot. This is an idyllic little place and the first natural pause in the walk. On from here, the footpath wends its way up the wilder looking Bretton Clough to a ruined farmhouse that the youngsters will want to investigate. In 1745, when this farmhouse was most probably occupied, Bretton Clough was used to hide cattle from Bonnie Prince Charlie's foraging Highlanders.

Uphill from the clough are the tiny hamlets of Nether Bretton and Bretton. The Barrel Inn is undoubtedly the nucleus of this little community. The building dates from 1637 and was a favourite haunt of lead miners in past centuries. Standing at 1300 feet above sea level, it is one of the highest pubs in the district. Because of its position on an escarpment overlooking the limestone plateau to the south, the view from here is outstanding. *continued on page 38*

Route 7

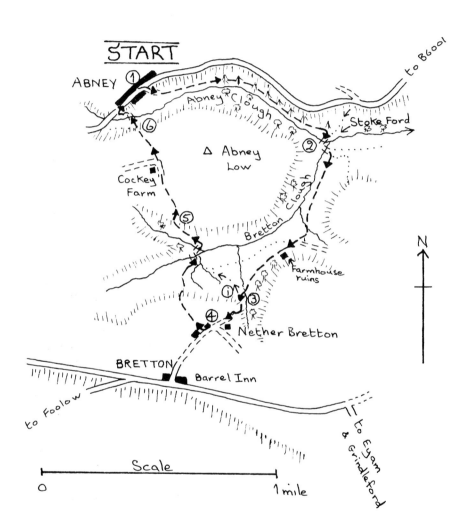

Abney Clough and Bretton   (Variation 3 miles)

START   *This walk can be started at Abney (G.R. 198798), further east above Stoke Ford (G.R. 213797), or as a last resort at Bretton (G.R. 201779). At either of the first two locations, there is space for only a handful of cars to park without inconvenience to village residents or to through traffic, which should be a consideration when planning this walk. To get to Abney, turn off the B.6001 from Hathersage to Grindleford opposite the Plough Inn. For Stoke Ford, stop immediately after passing through a plantation on the way to Abney. Park near the stile signposted Stoke Ford. To continue on to Bretton, go through Abney and turn left at the first junction, or approach the Hamlet from Foolow, near Eyam.*

ROUTE   As described from Abney.

1. *From the lowest point in the village, take the footpath leading to Abney Clough, which is signposted Eyam. Follow this down the valley on the left of the stream. After passing through a larch plantation, another path is joined at Stoke Ford.*

2. *Turn right and cross over two footbridges, then turn right again along the footpath signposted Bretton. Fork right in a short distance along the path that takes a gradually ascending line above Bretton Brook. Just after a steep rise, the ruins of a farmhouse are reached. Continue past this along a footpath with a hillside and disused quarry on the left. The footpath soon bends to the left and begins to ascend the left side of a gully. This leads to stile in the bed of the gully.*

3. *Cross the stile, then turn left and walk up the steep path to a gate and stile at the top. Continue over the stile and past a cottage to a track at Nether Bretton.*

4. *Turn right and follow the track for 50 metres to another cottage on the right. (For Bretton and the Barrel Inn, continue along the track, then retrace your steps to the cottage.) Turn right into the driveway, signposted Abney, and pass between the cottage and a ruined building. Cross a stile and head more or less straight down through fields to a marked stile. Continue down to the stream and cross two footbridges. Carry on up the other side of the valley to a stile.*

5. *Turn right and follow the wall on the right to another stile opposite Cockey Farm. Gain the track on the right of the farm. Where it bends left behind farm buildings the way is straight ahead by the wall on the*

On the way back to Abney, the footpath goes past Cockey Farm. As well as the ever present quagmire that has to be negotiated before an escape to pleasanter ground can be made, there is often the additional attraction of shire horses, whose inquisitiveness brings them to sniff out passers-by on the other side of the wall. To the east of the farm is Abney Low. The term 'low', or 'hlaw', is a word of Saxon origin denoting a 'heaped structure'. Many of these are the sites of Bronze Age barrows (burial mounds).

At various points en route, where the woods by the streams are more dense, a pair of binoculars would help in identifying some of the birdlife. Wood warbler and redstart, along with many other more common species can be seen hereabouts.

Refreshments Barrel Inn at Bretton. Children admitted, beer garden, snacks available.

---

right to a stile in this wall about 100 metres on. This section is usually badly churned and muddy, so it is best to take a wide sweep to the left. After crossing the stile, continue in the same general direction down to a gully.

6. *After crossing the gully, keep right and descend steep ground to a hidden stile. Continue over this and the stream in Abney Clough, then up to the road through Abney. Turn right to finish.*

SHORTER VARIATION
As for 1 and 2 above to the stile in the bed of the gully, then:

i. *instead of turning left after the stile, turn right and follow the footpath down the other side of the gully. This soon bears left, goes through gate posts, then leads directly to the two footbridges mentioned in 4 above. Continue as for 4 to 6 above.*

WHEATEAR
Black, white, buff, grey 15cm.

Route 8   6½ miles

(Shorter variation 3 miles)

Win Hill

Outline   Yorkshire Bridge ~ Win Hill ~ Killhill ~ Aston ~ Win Hill.

Summary   Although the easiest way up Win Hill is taken, the ascent from Yorkshire Bridge is close to 1000 feet - in other words, a fairly strenuous undertaking for those not used to hill walking. It is, nevertheless, a fine walk with some of the best views of the central Peak District, and takes in forest, open moorland, low-lying meadows and country lanes. Good, clear footpaths are followed up and off Win Hill, whence tracks and a short section of country lane lead to a well-stiled but little used footpath through fields. The last half mile descends along a path that forces a way through fairly dense natural vegetation that contrasts totally with the forested hillsides around.

Attractions   The walk starts just below the Ladybower Dam. Unlike many more modern dams, this and the other two dams in the Derwent Valley were built to blend as far as possible into the surroundings. The upper dam, Howden, was constructed in 1912, the Derwent in 1916 and Ladybower Dam was completed in 1945. The Howden and Derwent Dams were used during World War II for testing Dr. Barnes Wallis' bouncing bomb, and the film "The Dam Busters", telling this story, was also shot here. Before entering the forest just beyond the Ladybower Dam, make a point of stopping to show the youngsters the huge plug-hole which swallows up water when the level is high.

When the lakeside is left, the environment changes abruptly. The track wends its way up through larch and spruce plantation which creates an ambience more akin to Scandinavia than Derbyshire. In winter, after snow has fallen, this feeling is enhanced considerably. Looking from the track to the left, the forest is dense and, even on a bright day, a dark and murky place where little sunlight finds its way through to the barren forest floor.

Just as one is beginning to tire of being enclosed in the forest, the open heather clad upper slopes of Win Hill appear. This is the land of the curlew, the red grouse and the meadow pipit, the latter a small brown bird with white feathers in the tail. From the summit of Win Hill at 1523 feet above sea level, the view is panoramic and well worth the effort of the climb. The summit ridge also has built-in entertainment for the younger element, since it is rocky and provides plenty of scope for scrambling.

continued on page 42

39

Route 8

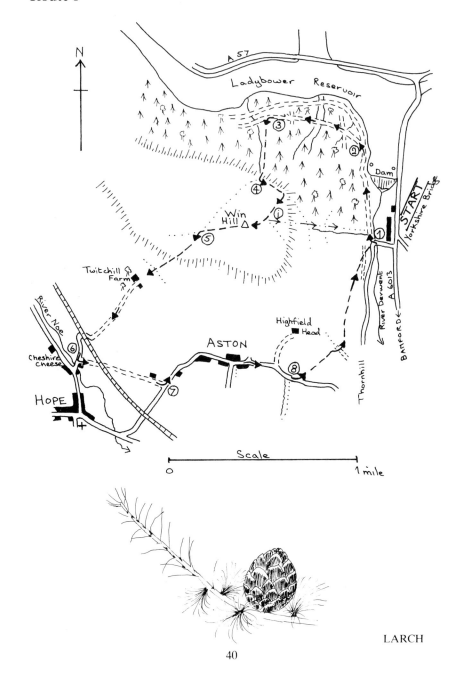

LARCH

40

Route 8   6½ miles

(Variation 3 miles)

Win Hill

START   *At Yorkshire Bridge, 1 mile north of Bamford on the A.6013. Take the road signposted to Thornhill, and park near the bridge. (G.R. 198849).*

ROUTE

1. *Walk up towards the dam and the reservoir by the track on the left of the river. On reaching the reservoir, continue past the overflow hole for 200 metres to a forest track ascending steeply to the left.*

2. *Take this track. In ¼ mile it is crossed by a gravel track with a culvert beneath. Keep straight on along a grassy track, passing over two more streams and another crossroads of tracks. Carry on as far as a turning point for vehicles a few metres before the track crosses another stream in a prominent gully.*

3. *Turn left at the turning point, and go directly uphill through the plantation. The footpath is vague for only a short distance but soon becomes more obvious. Continue to a gate at the top of the plantation. Win Hill summit is now directly ahead.*

4. *Turn left, and follow the narrow footpath as far as a wall going up the hillside towards the summit. Turn right and follow the footpath alongside the wall up to the top. Continue along and down the other side of the ridge as far as a left fork in the footpath.*

5. *Take this and descend steeply, crossing a stile on the way, to Twitchill Farm. Continue down along the farm track, under a railway bridge, and a little further to a cottage on the left. (To get to the Cheshire Cheese Inn, continue past the cottage and several others to the main road. The Inn is to the right. Retrace your steps to the cottage as described.)*

6. *Turn left at the track signposted Aston. Follow this to a minor road.*

7. *Turn left and walk along the road into and through the hamlet of Aston. In just under ½ mile from the highest point in the village, and 200 metres past a sharp right hand bend in the road, a footpath and stile on the right, signposted Hope, is reached. A few metres past this on the left is a less obvious wooden unmarked stile.*

8. *Cross this and bear right up through fields with stiles to the top corner of a field near the top edge of the wood facing. Follow the clearly marked footpath to the right past manholes enclosed by metal railings. This leads to a track of sorts. Go straight across and between two hawthorns*

Win Hill is a very windy place, even when there is not a trace of wind in the valley, and probably took its name from this fact. However, tradition has it that King Penda of Mercia won a battle against King Edwin of Northumbria in 632 A.D., and that the winner camped on Win Hill and the loser on Lose Hill across the Noe Valley. A more likely historical connection is with the Romans, for further west an old British track used by them crosses the ridge, providing a link between the fort of Navio, near Brough, and Melandra, near Glossop.

On the descent from Win Hill, a very steep grassy section above Twitchill Farm provides amusement, especially if the grass is wet. From the farm, a more gradual descent along a track leads to the hamlet of Killhill, from where a short diversion can be made to the Cheshire Cheese Inn.

Pleasant walking along a track, then a country lane, leads to the hamlet of Aston. A little further on, the lane is forsaken for a little used footpath which goes up through fields to a ridge from which there is a splendid view of the Ladybower Dam. The continuation is along a footpath that forces a way through wild shrubbery and tall bracken, providing interest for the naturalist and an adventurous half mile of descent for the youngsters.

Refreshments Cheshire Cheese Inn at Killhill near Hope. Children admitted, outside facilities, snacks available.

---

to a footpath which trends left downhill through shrubbery. Continue across a track near the bottom of the hill to finish at a stile by the bridge.

SHORTER VARIATION

i. *From the summit of Win Hill, retrace your steps to the wall and a prominent ladder stile. Continue straight down the hill along the footpath signposted Yorkshire Bridge. The path crosses a wide footpath and a stile before descending steeply on the left of a stream to the track where the walk started.*

ACCESS BY BUS

To Yorkshire Bridge, from Dronfield, Chesterfield and Castleton (Silver Service), daily; from Glossop and Sheffield (South Yorkshire), summer Sundays and Bank Holiday Monday.

Route 9

Back Tor and Lose Hill

Outline   Castleton ~ Back Tor ~ Lose Hill ~ Hope ~ Castleton.

Summary   Starting at the busiest place in the Peak District, the walk manages to avoid the more popular footpaths in the vicinity. A good introduction to hill walking, it takes in a part of the ridge dividing the Edale and Hope Valleys, the view from this ridge being undoubtedly one of the finest in the Peak. Well used tracks and footpaths are followed throughout, with a short section of road-walking in Hope. The way up to the ridge is mostly very gradual and becomes more strenuous only for the last third of a mile. From Back Tor, the footpath is followed to Lose Hill, with another few feet of ascent, then a rapid descent to Hope is made. The last section takes a riverside footpath back into Castleton.

Attractions   With a castle, four show caves, Blue John and the attraction of nearby Winnats Pass and Mam Tor, exploration of Castleton is best left for another day. A little history, however, will help provide a flavour of the place. Peveril Castle, together with the remains of a town ditch on its eastern perimeter, indicate that Castleton began as a Norman settlement in the 12th century, although the original wooden keep was erected by William Peveril towards the end of the 11th century. The castle was the seat of the Keeper of the Royal Forest of the Peak, through its importance declined in the 14th century with forest clearance for farming. By the 17th century, it was in ruins, the result being quarried for cottage building. In the 18th and 19th centuries the village was a lead-mining centre, and several relics are near at hand to investigate. Nowadays, the place thrives on its tourist trade, and the only mining is for the semi-precious bluish yellow - or bleu-jaune - stone known as Blue John.

On the first stretch of the walk out of Castleton, Mam Tor is seen at its best. Covered in snow, its east face resembles a miniature Eiger and in such conditions can provide interesting mountaineering up a cliff that is too dangerously loose at other times of the year. The name Mam Tor is Celtic in origin, meaning a peak in the shape of a woman's breast. On its summit are the earthwork remains of a Brigantian hillfort constructed between A.D. 50 and 70. Its most sensational function nowadays is as a launching pad for hang-gliders, a sport that has claimed several fatalities here. It is the updraught that attracts the pilots, and indeed the whole ridge to Lose Hill is a windy place because of its exposed position between two wide valleys.

continued on page 46

43

Route 9

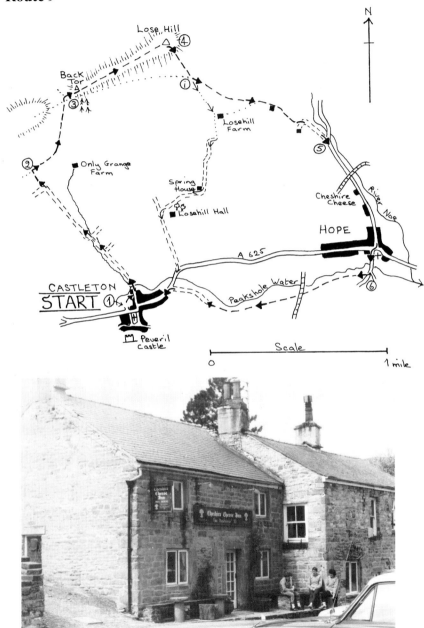

THE CHESHIRE CHEESE, HOPE

44

Route 9

5½ miles

(Variation 4 miles)

Back Tor and Lose Hill

START   *In Castleton, Back Street. This is the road on the right at the sharp left hand bend in the village coming from the direction of Hope. A footpath from the far right corner of the main car park leads directly to Back Street.*

ROUTE

1. *Follow the narrow lane out of the village, taking a left fork in just over ½ mile. Continue along the lane to where it bends sharp left. Leave it here, cross the stile straight ahead, and take the enclosed footpath, signposted Nether Booth. Continue up to stiles.*
2. *Turn right here, signposted Back Tor, and continue along the ascending footpath, bearing left at gateposts up steep ground to a stile on the ridge. Cross this and a footpath, then another stile.*
3. *Turn right and go up steeply to the top of Back Tor. Continue along the ridge footpath to Lose Hill.*
4. *Bear right at the summit down to a fence with two stiles. Continue down the main footpath. After crossing a stile, a steep descent leads down to the road linking Hope with Edale.*
5. *Turn right and walk along the road into Hope, passing the Cheshire Cheese en route. At the T-junction in the centre of Hope, turn right, then first left by the Woodroffe Arms. Continue over a bridge and uphill for about 150 metres to a stile on the right.*
6. *Cross the stile and follow the riverside footpath back to Castleton.*

SHORTER VARIATION   As for 1 to 3 above, then:

Go down from the summit to the two stiles. About 150 metres further on, a path joins from the right. Also, on the other side of the very broken wall immediately to the right is another footpath that leads down to Lose Hill Farm. Take this (i) to the stile immediately to the right of the farm. Follow the well signposted footpath and tracks back to Castleton.

ACCESS BY BUS

Numerous bus services to Castleton from east and west of the Peak District.

The footpath along the ridge follows an ancient packway linking Hope with Edale and Hayfield beyond. Why this high level route should have been preferred to a low level route through the Vale of Edale suggests this was originally the safer option, for one reason or another. The route joins this track at Back Tor. As with Mam Tor, its cliff is the result of a landslip. A closer look at the exposed rock reveals alternating layers of harder sandstone and soft shales. As the shales get washed away, stonefall occurs and Back Tor grows smaller. Eventually, the whole ridge will disappear in the process of erosion by rainwater. Further on is Lose Hill, the best viewpoint in these parts. To the north across the Edale Valley is the great bulk of Kinder Scout. South of the Hope and Derwent Valleys the lower lying Offerton, Bradwell and Abney Moors can be seen. And looking eastwards beyond Win Hill, the higher gritstone 'edges' can be made out.

On leaving Lose Hill, the next objective is refreshments at Hope, and it is all downhill. In medieval times, Hope was an important trading centre and still has a weekly stock market. On from here, the footpath back to Castleton follows the River Peakshole, which offers possibilities for waterside picnics and suchlike.

Refreshments At Hope, Cheshire Cheese. Children Admitted, beer garden, snacks available.

Woodroffe Arms. Large beer garden, snacks available, children admitted.

At Castleton, Bull's Head. Children admitted, beer garden, snacks available.

Castle Hotel. Children admitted, snacks available.

George Hotel. Beer garden, snacks available.

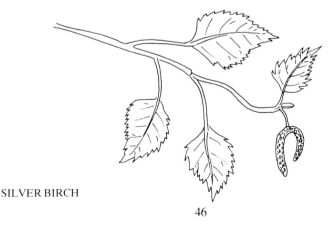

SILVER BIRCH

46

Route 10   5 miles

(Shorter variations 3½ miles)

Derwent Edge

Outline Cutthroat Bridge (A.57) ~ Derwent Edge ~ Lodge Cote ~ Ladybower Inn ~ Cutthroat Bridge.

Summary A good introduction to moorland walking, it follows well worn footpaths, covers varied terrain and is rewarded with fine views. Although not as serious a proposition as Route 11 it is advised that the leader of the party carries map and compass and can use them to a reasonable degree of proficiency. As with other exposed moorland walks, there is little in the way of shelter from the weather on the higher ground, so that adequate preparations should be made to keep the party warm and dry come what may. Starting at Cutthroat Bridge, a gradual ascent over 2 miles is made to Derwent Edge. From here, a walk along the Edge to see the weathered tors follows, after which steps are retraced and a descent made to a track passing through a Nature Reserve that overlooks Ladybower Reservoir. The track winds round to the Ladybower Inn, climbs a little, then levels out before reaching Cutthroat Bridge.

Attractions The walk starts at Cutthroat Bridge, which seems to have acquired its gruesome name because in the 16th century at an older bridge a little further upstream a man was found with his throat cut. Beyond the bridge is wide open space without walls or fences. The lower slopes of the moor are covered in a mixture of grass, bilberry and bracken which give way to heather on the higher ground. In spring, the bilberry has an orange tinge which is striking in bright sunlight. When the berries are ripe, it is tempting to stop and gather but this is not open access country, and any fruit picking should be by the footpath only.

The rich heathery slopes are cultured through controlled burning of the plant in spring to ensure the continued breeding of red grouse which, in turn, attract sportsmen from all over the world to come and shoot. Thus, grouse shooting has tended to conserve such moors as there are, for without the substantial income arising from shooting rights the land would undoubtedly have been given over to other forms of farming more destructive of the natural vegetation. A reminder that this is shooting country is the presence of shooting butts lining the footpath. These have a certain fascination for children but are also handy as wind breaks should the need arise.

continued on page 50

D   47

Route 10

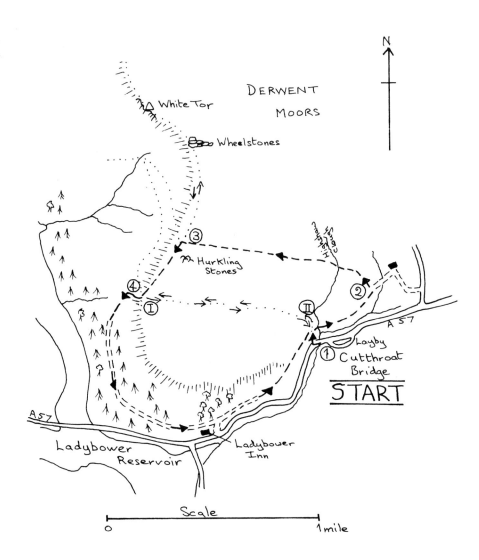

N

DERWENT
MOORS

White Tor

Wheelstones

③

Hurkling
Stones

④

Ⅰ

Ⅱ

②

A 57

Layby

① Cutthroat
Bridge

START

A57

Ladybower
Reservoir

Ladybower
Inn

Scale

0   1mile

Route 10   5 miles
(Variations 3½ miles each)
Derwent Edge

START   *Park at a lay-by on the Sheffield side of Cutthroat Bridge, which is about a mile northeast of the Ladybower Inn on the A.57. (G.R. 214874).*

ROUTE

1. *Pass through a handgate on the north side of the road at Cutthroat Bridge. Follow the footpath for 50 metres or so, then cross the stream to the right of the path. Another footpath leads on from here parallel to the stream by the A.57 heading eastwards. Continue along this to a gate.*

2. *Turn left after the gate and follow the wall uphill. This footpath crosses Highshaw Clough and eventually leads up on to Derwent Edge and the footpath that goes along the edge. (For the detour to the Wheelstones, turn right, and walk along the edge for about ½ mile. Retrace your steps.)*

3. *Turn left here (or continue in the same direction past the crossroads if returning from the Wheelstones) and follow the edge footpath down to the next crossroads.*

4. *Turn right at this point and descend steeply to a track. Follow the track left along the top edge of a plantation, through a Nature Reserve, and on to a point immediately above and behind the Ladybower Inn. (Access is by a track which doubles back down to the road about 100 metres past the Inn.) Continue from here along the same track, which at first climbs above woods and a quarry. In levelling out, the track becomes a footpath for the last ½ mile back to Cutthroat Bridge.*

SHORTER VARIATIONS

I   *As for 1 to 3 above, then: Turn left at the crossroads instead of right, and follow the footpath back down to Cutthroat Bridge. (3½ miles).* **OR**

II *Start as for 1 above but instead of crossing the stream, continue along the main footpath as it bends to the left. Follow this up to a crossroads on Derwent Edge. Go straight across and continue as for 4 above. (3½ miles).*

ACCESS BY BUS

To Ladybower Inn from Sheffield (South Yorkshire) summer Sundays and Bank Holiday Monday; from Barnsley (South Yorkshire), summer Sundays and Bank Holiday Monday.

On reaching Derwent Edge, the land drops away sharply to reveal a magnificent view of the upper Derwent Valley and the hills and moors beyond. Indeed, the whole scene has been likened to a miniature Lake District. The Edge itself forms part of a gritstone escarpment that stretches for miles southwards and includes Bamford, Stanage, Froggatt, Curbar and Chatsworth Edges. Along Derwent Edge erosion has left stumps of gritstone which wind, water and sand have shaped into weird natural sculptures reminiscent of Henry Moore's work. Some of these closely resemble man-made artefacts, hence such names as the Salt Cellar, the Cakes of Bread, and the Wheelstones. The latter, also known as the Coach and Horses, is the nearest of these and is an ideal spot for lunch; the youngsters can play and scramble around on the rocks whilst the adults can amuse themselves identifying the hills and other landmarks in the distance.

The steep heathery slope below the Edge is the haunt of the mountain or blue hare, which, like the red grouse, was introduced for sport. Early in the year, they can usually be spotted quite easily for their white winter coats often moult less quickly than the snow melts.

On leaving the Edge, a pleasant track along the top edge of a plantation which is also a Nature Reserve leads easily round to the Ladybower Inn, where refreshments can be taken. Along this section, tall bracken fringes the footpath, providing entertainment for the younger element. Once at the Inn or on the banks of Ladybower across the road, if the party is feeling too relaxed to continue, it is not far for the driver to go and retrieve the transport.

Refreshments Ladybower Inn. Children admitted, beer garden, snacks available.

MOUNTAIN HARE

Fairbrook Naze and Kinder Edge

Outline   Snake Inn (A.57) ~ Fair Brook ~ Fairbrook Naze ~ Kinder Edge ~ Ashop Clough ~ Snake Path ~ Snake Inn.

(not recommended for children under 9)

Summary   This and the other suggested walks on Kinder should only be attempted by parties led by someone proficient and experienced in high moorland terrain and skilled in the use of map and compass. The route follows a footpath, narrow and exposed in parts, up the deep gully cut by Fair Brook. The last few hundred feet is the steepest. On reaching the summit plateau, the most adventuruous way is to head directly for Kinder Edge on a compass bearing, although it is easier to walk around the edge, where navigation is somewhat more straightforward. Going the direct route, though only ¾ mile the walking is strenuous amongst the peat groughs, and there is neither footpath nor landmark. Once Kinder Edge is reached, a steep but mainly grassy descent, again without footpath, is made to Ashop Clough, where a likely place has to be selected to cross the wide stream. From here, the Snake Path, demanding care over a fifty metre section, is followed back to the A.57 near the Snake Inn. For a party with a competent leader, this is a fine walk as well as being one of the shortest routes up Kinder.

Attractions   Starting at 1000 feet above sea level, with only just over a mile and a half to the summit plateau of Kinder, the walk described is well suited for parties with youngsters in tow. On leaving the road, the footpath immediately delves into the half-light of a plantation, only to leave it just as abruptly at a footbridge suspended high above the River Ashop. In another few minutes, the deep narrow gully formed by Fair Brook is entered. The footpath follows the stream up to the top, which is clearly in sight for most of the ascent. The gully is itself a most attractive feature, its stream following a twisting course over a succession of waterfalls at the base of which pools have formed. As height is gained and the steep rocky terrain of Fairbrook Naze is approached, the scene is more akin to mountain than moorland. Scrambling up the bed of the boulder-strewn gully for the last two or three hundred feet further enhances this and provides added interest when the young ones are tiring of the uphill grind.

Once on the top, the scene changes dramatically, for the eye is met with what looks like a vast, flat expanse of moorland. The walk across

continued on page 54

Route 11

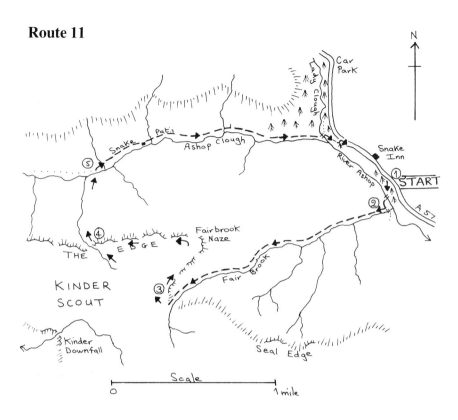

LADYBOWER

Route 11   5 miles

Fairbrook Naze and Kinder Edge

START   *There is limited parking space along the A.57 about 300 to 400 metres down from the Snake Inn. Get there early to avoid disappointment. (G.R. 115903). An alternative start can be made from a car park ½ mile north of the Snake Inn. This would add a mile to the journey.*

ROUTE

1. *A stile gives access to a footpath which descends through the plantation on the south side of the A.57. This leads to a footbridge over the River Ashop. Follow the footpath left after the footbridge as far as the confluence of Fair Brook with the River Ashop.*
2. *Turn right and follow the footpath alongside Fair Brook to the top.*
3. *From here, take a bearing and head for a point about midway along 'The Edge', where it is cleft by a stream (G.R. 086897). Alternatively, follow the edge round to the same point.*
4. *Keeping just right of the gully and stream, go more or less straight down to Ashop Clough. Cross the stream at a convenient place to gain the Snake Path on the opposite bank. Paddling can be safer than jumping stones.*
5. *Follow the Snake Path downstream, crossing the footbridge over Lady Clough, and on up to the road a little way from the Snake Inn. Turn right to finish.*

Two other suggestions for short walks on Kinder

From Edale:

i   *Take the Pennine Way to the top of Grinds Brook. Follow it towards Crowden Head for about ½ mile or so, then bear off this to Crowden Tower. Descend to the stream and a footpath on the other side. Follow this down for about ¾ mile, then branch off to the left above a wood. Continue round to Edale.*

ii *From the top of Grinds Brook, head for Grindslow Knoll (110867) and follow the well-used footpath down to Edale. Alternatively, walk round to Ringing Rodger (127873), then descend to the Pennine Way footpath to return to Edale.*

here, however, is anything but flat. The area is riddled with peat groughs (drainage channels). Negotiating these, some of which are 12 feet deep, presents a ready made assault course as well as keeping the one with the compass totally occuppied in steering a straight course, however clear the conditions. Fortunately, the crossing to Kinder Edge is only ¾ mile, and the excitement provided by the groughs tends to maintain enthusiasm over the distance.

The peat, up to twenty feet thick in places, is formed mainly of sphagnum moss and was 7000 years in the making. The sphagnum grows only in isolated bogs nowadays because of the effects of air pollution from the industrial zones to the west of the moors. Nowadays, the vegetation cover is mainly moorland grasses and ling heather.

On reaching Kinder Edge, a steep scramble downhill leads to easier ground and Ashop Clough. There are no footbridges here, so that initiative is called for in crossing the wide, though shallow stream. As a last resort, this can provide a good excuse for cooling the feet. The last section follows the Snake Path down Ashop Clough. An old shooting cabin, now in ruins, and several likely spots for pausing and waterside activities are passed en route.

Not forgetting the wildlife, on the higher ground the red grouse is usually sighted. In spring and summer, such migrants as the dunlin, golden plover and meadow pipit breed alongside the grouse. And high among the rock cloughs, where it nests, the ring ouzel is occasionally seen. Keep an eye out for mountain hare below Kinder Edge.

Refreshments Snake Inn. Children admitted, beer garden, snacks available.

ACCESS BY BUS
To Snake Inn from Glossop and Sheffield (South Yorkshire), summer Sundays and Bank Holiday Monday; from Manchester, Stockport and Glossop (Greater Manchester), summer Sundays and Bank Holidays.

Route 12

White Brow and Middle Moor from Hayfield

Outline   Hayfield ~ Farlands Booth ~ White Brow ~ Little Hayfield ~ Hayfield.

Summary   A pleasant walk combining riverside with a dash of Kinder. An easy footpath is followed alongside the River Sett as far as Kinder Reservoir, then a short steep ascent is made to Middle Moor at 1100 feet above sea level. This is directly opposite Kinder Downfall and must be one of the best vantage points for viewing the amphitheatre at whose centre it lies. A half-mile of easy moorland footpath follows, from which a descent is made along a public right of way that has become disused. What vestige of a footpath remains is overgrown with heather over a half mile section. However, a prominent gully with a stream which flows to the same point the route is headed acts as marker. Tracks and footpaths are then followed via Little Hayfield back to the start. The shorter variation misses out the overgrown section as well as Little Hayfield and returns by the well-used Snake Path more directly to Hayfield.

Attractions   Hayfield is an attractive settlement that developed around a textile industry in the 19th century. Before the Industrial Revolution, however, Hayfield was an assembly point for the 'jaggers' and their teams of twenty or thirty horses or mules. From the Packhorse Inn, some would set off on the long journey to Holmfirth, whilst others would be headed via Edale Cross to the Vale of Edale and settlements to the east of the moors. The Packhorse Inn, like the George Inn, probably dates from the 16th century, and several cottages and former farm buildings were built at this time. It was from Hayfield that a mass trespass on the grouse moors of Kinder took place in 1932, leading to arrests and imprisonment in some cases. Public access was eventually granted in 1949 after a prolonged campaign.

Leaving the village behind, the walk alongside the tree-lined River Sett is a delight. Several interesting old cottages are passed en route, the last of these at Farlands booth. A 'booth' was a temporary shed or shelter used by herdsmen on land that was enclosed to keep out wolves. Farlands, and other Booths in the Vale of Edale, were Tudor cattle ranches.

Just before reaching the dam of Kinder Reservoir, a steep though short ascent is made to the top of White Brow, beyond which the rest is

continued on page 58

Route 12

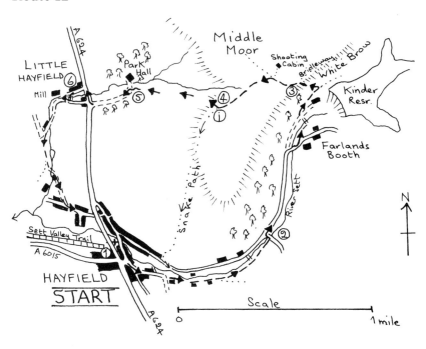

HAYFIELD

Route 12   **4 miles**

White Brow and Middle Moor from Hayfield

START   *At Hayfield car park/bus station, which is situated at the eastern end of the Sett Valley Trail and across the road from the main part of the village.* (G.R. 035869)

ROUTE

1. *From the car park, take the underpass into the village. Turn right and walk up the main street. Bear left at the top into Valley Road. Follow this to its end, where it becomes a track. Continue along this, then a footpath on the right bank of the river. Keep on the riverside footpath, passing a campsite on the right, until a minor road is joined.*

2. *Turn left to go over a bridge, then right. Follow the road for ½ mile to another road bridge. Cross it and leave it straight away for a footpath, again on the right bank of the river. This leads to a footbridge. After crossing the footbridge, cross the stile next to the entrance to the water works buildings and Mountain Rescue Post. Follow the ascending footpath for 300 metres, then turn left along another footpath which goes up steeply to the top of White Brow. At the top, another footpath is joined at a 'Bridleway' sign.*

3. *Bear left along this to a fork in 200 metres. Take the left fork, signposted Hayfield. Follow this for ⅓ mile to a point halfway between the corner of a wall on the left and a gateway straight ahead.*

4. *Bear right down a heathery slope (no footpath in evidence). Continue in this general direction, keeping above a gully and stream. Head towards the point where the stream enters a wood. There is also a high wall at this point.*

5. *Follow the wall left to a gate. Go through the gate and turn left down a track (Park Hall is on the immediate right). Follow this to the main road from Hayfield to Glossop. Turn right at the main road to The Lantern Pike.*

6. *Walk down the road adjacent to the inn to a footbridge opposite a row of cottages. Cross it and continue along a track, passing an old mill and another row of cottages, to where it doubles back to the right. Leave the track at the bend, and go straight on along a footpath that clings to the top edge of a wood with duck ponds below. Ignore any rightwards possiblities. Descend to old farm buildings by a stream, then continue along a track to a minor road in Hayfield. Turn left to join the main street in the village.*

downhill. Before going over the brow, take a look at the rather magnificent scenery hereabouts. Across the valley is the craggy cleft of Kinder Downfall, made all the more impressive because of its position at the centre of a huge natural amphitheatre that drops 1000 feet to the reservoir below. A wide-angled lens to transport the scene back home, and binoculars for picking out detail and people around the Downfall would be useful here. The name Kinder Scout probably derives from the old Norse "Kyndur", meaning water, and "scuti", meaning a projecting cliff - a rather apt description of the topography of the Downfall.

Beyond White Brow, the scene unfolds in the opposite direction. Due west across the valley is Lantern Pike, and further north Cown Edge Rocks can be seen. Walking across Middle Moor, whilst only on the fringe of Kinder, provides a taste of what is higher. Near a shooting hut and not far off route is a well-signposted "Dangerous Bog" that is the nearest to a swamp to be found in these parts. A footbridge across it enables closer scrutiny. It is also a good place for the 'young' ones to toss in the odd stone to see what happens to it.

If the route to Little Hayfield is taken, the descent from the moor, whilst a little off-putting to adults, tends to have the opposite effect on youngsters as they pioneer their way over uneven ground trying to locate a footpath concealed by deep heather. Just as this is becoming wearisome, the heather boundary is reached and so is easier ground amongst rhododendrons. This is a mandatory stop for exploring, hiding and other adventurous or fantasy pursuits before refreshments at the Lantern Pike.

The last section down the valley to Hayfield provides a pleasant contrast to what has gone before.

Refreshments Lantern Pike, Little Hayfield. Beer garden, snacks.

Packhorse Inn, Hayfield. Children admitted, beer garden & snacks available.

Cafe in Hayfield.

———————

SHORTER VARIATION   As for 1 to 3 above, then:
i. *Continue through the gateway and follow the Snake Footpath more directly back into Hayfield.*

ACCESS BY BUS
To Hayfield from Stockport and Glossop (Greater Manchester), daily.

(Shorter variation 4 miles)
Windgather Rocks and the Dale of Goyt

Outline Whaley Bridge ~ Taxal Moor ~ Windgather Rocks ~ Overton ~ Shallcross Wood ~ Whaley Bridge.

Summary Starting in Whaley Bridge, the walk climbs out of the valley in stages to reach the ridge where the appropriately named Windgather Rocks are situated. From this high point there are extensive views of the high moors and hills to the east. From Windgather, the footpath makes a short descent through pinewoods before climbing to the top of a second, lower-lying ridge overlooking the Dale of Goyt, which is the next objective. Once down in the valley, a short diversion, though uphill, can be made to the Shady Oak Inn at Fernilee. The continuation is by a footpath which runs alongside the River Goyt through wild, unspoilt woodland. A short section of walking alongside a main road only briefly interrupts the riverside walk back into Whaley Bridge.

Attractions Many people pass through Whaley Bridge en route to other destinations but few contemplate stopping off here, and their experience of the town is limited to the development alongside the A.6. Off the main road in either direction, however, there are hidden charms. Many of its old stone cottages and inns date from the 19th century, when Whaley Bridge grew as a cotton town. The terminal basin of the Peak Forest Canal, now restored and with narrow boats for hire, is well worth a visit. It is here that the notorious Cromford and High Peak Railway used to end, having attained a height of 1264 feet above sea level at Hurdlow, 2 miles west of Monyash (G.R. 1167). An old iron railway bridge at the back of the car park, used nowadays as a footbridge, brought the line over the river to the canal terminal. The minerals transported from Cromford along this line continued their journey by barge from Whaley Bridge.

The walk out from the town passes beneath the concrete Toddbrook Dam. Once up alongside the reservoir, the scene becomes much more attractive, and a few minutes can be spent watching the sailing boats.

In gradual stages, the walk follows a combination of tracks, footpaths and country lanes to reach Taxal Edge. Buildings give way to grassland, coniferous plantation, and eventually to moorland vegetation as one nears Taxal Edge, only to return once more to grassland on the western slopes.

continued on page 63

59

Route 13

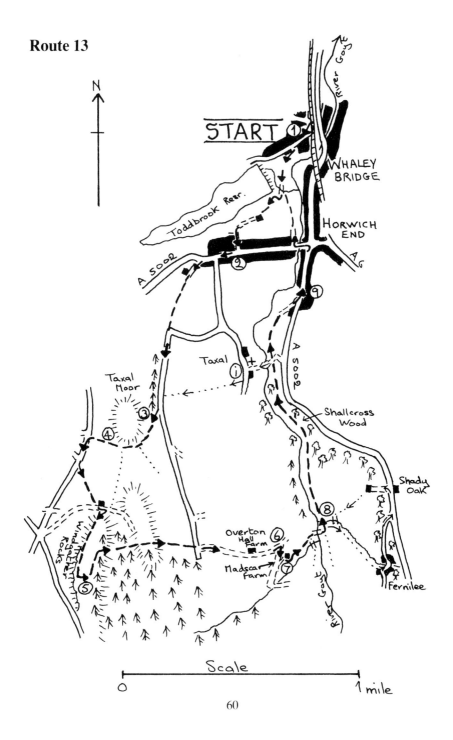

Scale

0   1 mile

60

Route 13

6 miles

(Variation 4 miles)

Windgather Rocks and the Dale of Goyt

START   *At Whaley Bridge, or at Taxal if the shorter walk is selected. Taxal is situated 1½ miles south of Whaley Bridge and is reached from the A.5002 at Horwich End.* (G.R. 006798).

ROUTE

1. *The walk starts on Reservoir Road near the railway station. Continue under the railway bridge and straight on as far as an old chapel on the left. Branch left off the road behind the chapel to a playground. Continue over a footbridge, then zigzag up to the right. The footpath leads up to the left side of the dam. Continue alongside the reservoir to a farm. Pass through the farm and follow a track to the end of a street. Walk along the street to a main road (A.5002).*

2. *Turn right, and walk uphill to a sharp righthand bend, where a tarmac drive forks off the main road up to the left. Follow this to a gateway and stile. Cross the stile and continue along a footpath to another stile at a minor road. Go straight on, passing a stile on the left signposted Taxal, and continue to the edge of the plantation on the right of the road.*

3. *Bear right uphill at this point. Continue past rhododendrons to more open ground and, eventually, a gap in the ridge. Once through the gap, there are two possibilities, although the second of these is* **not** *a public right of way.*

4. *The legitimate route is straight ahead and downhill to a minor road. Turn left and walk along the road to the first stile on the left. Cross over this and bear right up through fields to a stile and a track. Go left along the track to an old farm building. A few metres past this on the right is an open gateway. Turn right here and follow the wall on the right up the ridge to Windgather Rocks. (The second possibility from the gap is to go left through a handgate, then to follow the wall on the right to the farm track mentioned above. Turn right here and continue to the open gateway by the farm, then continue up the ridge to Windgather.) Access to the rocks is on the right before a wall with a stile.*

5. *To continue, cross the aforementioned stile and turn left. Walk down to the edge of a plantation. The footpath goes left here. Follow it along the top of the plantation. Where the fence on the right of the footpath turns right, follow it through pines down into a dell and up again to a stile. Continue up to the top of a ridge overlooking the Dale of Goyt, then straight down the other side, keeping more or less parallel with the edge*

of the plantation on the right. Cross a tarmac track, then a cattle grid, and follow a farm track down to Overton Hall Farm.

6. *About 250 metres past the farm, the main track doubles back downhill to the right. Continue along this to another farm on the left (Madscar Farm).*

7. *Leave the track at this point. Walk up the farm drive and pass through two gates on the immediate right of the building. The footpath, which is vague beyond the second gate, is signposted Hillbridge. Bear right downhill and follow posts with yellow arrow markings. The footpath becomes more obvious as it bears left down to a footbridge.*

8. *After crossing the footbridge over the River Goyt, turn left to follow the riverside footpath. This leads into Shallcross Wood and, eventually, to a track. (Turn left here to go into Taxal on the other side of the river.) Otherwise, cross the track and continue along the footpath on the right of the river. This leads to a main road (A.5002).*

9. *Turn left and walk down past a garage to a road junction. Turn left again along the Macclesfield road. Follow it across the river, then turn right into Goyt Road. Continue through the park to finish on Reservoir Road.*

(If a visit to the Shady Oak is to be included, after crossing the footbridge as for 8 above, turn left but bear right almost immediately to a solitary oak tree. Follow the grassy footpath up to a stile, ignoring a footbridge on the left, and continue uphill alongside a hedge, with stiles acting as markers. Go through a farm gate, then left along a track between buildings in the tiny hamlet of Fernilee. Continue to a main road (A.5002), and follow this to the Shady Oak Inn. From the Inn, take the track opposite down to a farm. Go through the farm to a stile, cross it and continue to another stile (muddy). Carry on to the footbridge ignored on the way up, and rejoin the main route.)

SHORTER VARIATION

i. *Starting at Taxal, from the car park walk past the church to gateway and stile on the right, signposted Taxal Edge. Continue straight up the hill to join the longer walk at the stile mentioned in 2 above.*

ACCESS BY BUS

To Whaley Bridge from Manchester, Stockport, New Mills, Chesterfield and Mansfield (East Midland/Lincolnshire/Silver Service), daily; from Buxton and Stockport (Trent), daily; from Macclesfield and New Mills (Crosville), daily.

The next objective, and clearly visible, is Windgather Rocks. The legendary rock-climber, Joe Brown, cut his teeth here as a youth, and the gritstone crag is an excellent training ground for beginners. For those who might fancy a bit of easy scrambling or low level 'bouldering', there are one or two places at the extreme ends of the crag where this can be done in relative safety, under supervision.

The walk back through the secluded natural woodland bordering the River Goyt is in total contrast to what has gone before. The wide variety of trees and shrubs that grow here attract several interesting species of birds. On and by the river, dipper, common sandpiper and grey wagtail may be seen, whilst amongst the oak and birch trees redstart and wood warbler are often sighted. This woodland is what remains of a medieval forest that stretched eastwards towards Sherwood.

Just off route, unless the shorter walk is taken, is Taxal, a secluded and attractive little hamlet set in picturesque surroundings and certainly worth a visit. It was a settlement as far back as the 13th century. Its church, though marred by Victorian "restorers", has a battlemented tower, parts of which date back to the 16th century at least. In the churchyard is an ancient yew tree that is said to be as old as the original church. Given the quaintness of the place as a whole, it seems a pity that the inn had to become a private residence.

Refreshments Shady Oak, Fernilee. Children admitted, grass banking for outside drinking, snacks available.

Mobile tea-shop, in a layby on the A.5002 adjacent to Taxal.

GOYT VALLEY

PANNIER'S BRIDGE

Route 14

Three Shire Heads from Flash

Outline   Flash ~ Hilltop ~ Black Clough ~ Knar ~ Wicken Walls ~ Flash.

Summary   The area covered by the walk, whilst never spectacular, has an atmosphere and attractiveness deriving from its remote situation. Footpaths, tracks and country lanes which were once packhorse trails are followed through moorland and valley that, in past centuries, supported a larger rural population than today, if the many ruins are anything to go by. At several points along the route, there are splendid views of the dramatic hills surrounding. The walk takes in Three Shire Heads, a beautiful spot where Derbyshire, Staffordshire and Cheshire meet at the confluence of two streams which are the source of the River Dane. The walking itself is never arduous but the last ½ mile along a road back into Flash is uphill.

Attractions   A product of the 18th century, Flash has been described as a "harsh village of weatherworn cottages". Given its altitude at 1518 feet above sea level, its harsh winter climate and its remoteness, it is hardly surprising that it should take on this aspect. In the past, Flash had a reputation for manufacturing forged or 'Flash' money, and the moors and valleys to the west of the village provided ideal cover for the local bandits when the law was on their tail. In addition to its infamous past, it lays claim to being the highest village in the U.K.

On leaving Flash, the route makes its way over moorland. Broken walls, disused tracks and the odd ruin suggest this area was once farmed more earnestly. To the west of the footpath is Wolf Edge. In medieval times, wolves did inhabit the then wooded valleys in the vicinity. Because of the remoteness of the area, some of the less commonly seen species of moorland bird, such as the curlew, snipe and the golden plover, may be sighted. And the wheatear, a bird the size of a chaffinch with a distinctive white rump, is usually seen bobbing and flitting about, chasing flies.

A short diversion to Hilltop is worth it, for the extensive view over the limestone country to the east. Also, two of the Peak District's major rivers, the Manifold and the Dove, start their courses within 1½ miles of each other, the former to the south of Hilltop and the latter to the north.

Pleasant walking along narrow country lanes lead down to Black Clough and, a little further, Pannier's Bridge at Three Shire Heads. This wild and beautiful spot, with its two old packhorse bridges and a tumbling

continued on page 68

Route 14

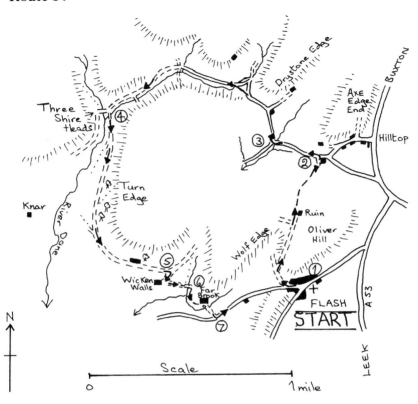

REDSTART
Red, black and grey 4cm.

Route 14   4½ miles

Three Shire Heads from Flash

START   *The walk is described from Flash, just off the A.53 from Leek to Buxton.* (G.R. 025672).

ROUTE

1. *Walk past the front of the New Inn and, a little further on, a former Wesleyan chapel on the right. Continue to the first track on the right, and follow it to a fork in ¼ mile. Take the right fork, and continue to where the track ends at the ruins of a building, ignoring a walled track to the left. Walk straight past the ruins and bear slightly left across two fields to a stile in the corner of the second of these. Once over the stile, head for a boundary stone directly ahead. Continue past this to a makeshift stile in the fence on the right. Climb over it and continue down a track to an old farm building on a country lane. (For the view of the limestone country, turn right here and take the first left into Hilltop, then retrace your steps.)*

2. *Turn left and follow the lane for ¼ mile to a T-junction.*

3. *Turn right and continue along this road, ignoring any other possibilities. As it begins to descend to the right into a valley with a stream, leave it to follow a wall on the left, thus cutting a corner. Turn left and continue along the same road with a stream on the left. The tarmac soon gives way to a rough track. This eventually leads down to Pannier's Bridge at Three Shire Heads. Do not cross the bridge.*

4. *Turn left and walk downstream on the left bank of the River Dane. In a few hundred metres, the track forks. Take the upper track and follow this, as it bends to the left, for a mile, passing cottages on the way. Immediately below and to the right of the track is Wicken Walls Farm.*

5. *Turn sharp right along the track leading to the farm, then head for a gate and stile on the left of the buildings. After crossing the stile, continue along a disused walled track to a footbridge.*

6. *Cross the footbridge and turn right. The path becomes a track at another farm (Far Brook). Follow it to a minor road.*

7. *Turn left at the road and walk steeply uphill back to Flash.*

ACCESS BY BUS
To Traveller's Rest, near Flash, from Leek and Reapsmoor (Clowes), Monday to Friday only.

stream with waterfalls and pools, is both a natural place to pause and the walk's central attraction for children. Wandering downstream from here, look on the river for grey wagtail and dipper.

On the last leg of the journey, take time to sample the views southwards of the Dane Valley, the jagged outline of Ramshaw Rocks, and the prominent high ridge of the Roaches and Hen Cloud.

Refreshments New Inn at Flash. Children admitted, beer garden, snacks available.

RAMSHAW ROCKS   Route 16

(Shorter variation 4 miles)

Lud's Church and the Dane Valley

Outline Danebridge ~ Hangingstone Farm ~ Roach End ~ Lud's Church ~ Back Dane ~ Danebridge.

Summary A fine walk full of contrast in one of the most secluded corners of the Peak District. Obvious footpaths and tracks are followed throughout, and there is plenty of interest en route for children. From Danebridge in the Dane Valley an ascent is made to the ridge flanking the River Dane on its south side. Apart from a short section early on amidst pinewoods, the ascent is mostly gradual. If the longer walk is taken, the ridge is followed to a road pass at Roach End, then a descent is made to a forest, wherein lies the curious phenomenon of Lud's Church. A further descent through the forest leads to the foot of the Dane Valley. This very attractive dale, with its pure, fast flowing river, is then followed back into Danebridge.

Attractions Soon out of the quaint little hamlet of Danebridge, the footpath delves into pinewoods and climbs out steeply to gain a track at Hangingstone Farm. The farm takes its name from a prominent overhanging gritstone cliff perched on the ridge 300 metres further on. Hanging Stone carries two plaques, one of which reveals the mystery of the wallabies said to be roaming in the Roches Estate. A footpath leads off the track to it for those who seek to satisfy their curiosity.

   A half a mile on from the farm, a public footpath crosses the ridge. At this point, a concessionary footpath along the ridge can be followed for about 1½ miles. This is in a splendid position, and the views both north and southwards are outstanding. Looking south eastwards along the ridge, the crags of the Roaches and Hen Cloud can be clearly discerned, and stretching out below them is Tittesworth Reservoir and the area around Leek. Looking northwards beyond the Dane Valley is the prominent peak of Shutlingsloe, and northeast is Axe Edge, beyond which lies the White Peak. On the northern slopes of the ridge the rarer black grouse breeds alongside the red grouse. This is also curlew country, and whinchat and snipe may be sighted along this stretch.

   On leaving the ridge, a forest of scots pine is entered. There are many of the more common woodland species of bird here but go quietly and you may see crossbill, which tend to move around in flocks. Deep in the woods and alongside the footpath is Lud's Church, a 60 foot deep

continued on page 72

Route 15

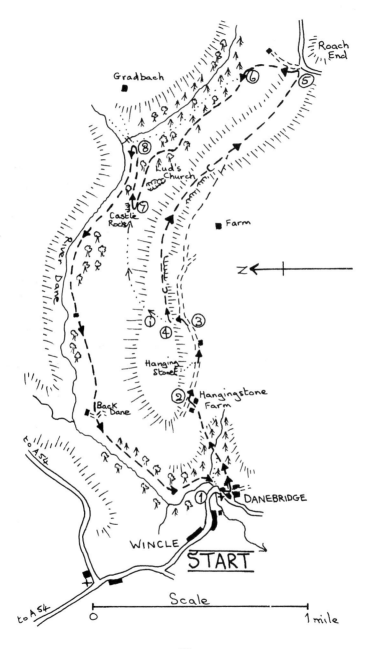

Roach End

Gradbach

Lud's Church

Castle Rocks

River Dane

Farm

Hanging Stones

Back Dane

Hangingstone Farm

DANEBRIDGE

WINCLE

START

to A 54

to A 54

Scale

0   1 mile

70

Route 15   6 miles

(Variation 4 miles)

Lud's Church and the Dane Valley

START   *At Wincle, roughly midway between Congleton and Buxton and south off the A.54 (G.R. 964652). Park opposite the gate to the trout farm about 200 metres on the Wincle side of the River Dane.*

ROUTE

1. *Walk over the bridge to Danebridge. Ignoring the first signposted footpath immediately after crossing the bridge, continue up the road as far as a chapel on the right. Opposite this, on the left, is a footpath signposted Back Forest and Gradbach. Follow this up between houses to a drive. Turn left and continue to a stile on the right of a house. Cross this and walk parallel to the fence on the left, to the wood facing. The footpath becomes more obvious at this point. Continue through the wood and across a stream, then up more steeply to the top of the wood and a stile. Carry on through a field to the farm ahead (Hangingstone Farm). Walk through the farm, as signposted, to join a track at a higher level.*

2. *Turn right and follow the track for ⅓ mile to a gate and stile. The Roaches Estate is entered at this point. (A public footpath continues straight on from here, at first using the track but eventually coming up to the top of the ridge to join the route as described in section 4.)*

3. *After the stile, go left up a track to the top of the ridge. Cross a stile by a gate.*

4. *Turn right after the stile and follow the concessionary footpath going up the ridge, which is signposted Roach End. In 1½ miles, the footpath meets a minor road at Roach End.*

5. **Before** *crossing the stile leading to the road, turn left and descend along a rough footpath on the immediate left of a wall, on the other side of which a track runs down to a farm. The footpath leads to the edge of a pine forest.*

6. *Turn left immediately on entering the forest and continue along a footpath which keeps close to the forest-moorland divide. Take a right fork in about half a mile and, about 300 metres further on, look for the entrance to Lud's Church on the immediate left of the footpath. Continue to a junction, next to which are Castle Rocks.*

7. *Turn right and descend along a footpath to the River Dane.*

chasm more than 150 metres long brought about by landslip. It has a mysterious atmosphere and is supposed to be the legendary Green Chapel of the medieval poem "Sir Gawain and the Green Knight". However, it is more likely that the place took its name from Walter de Ludank. A follower of John Wycliffe, a religious reformer in the reign of Richard II, he held secret services here. Whilst exploration of the chasm is interesting, wandering about above it should be discouraged. There are no fences, and a fall would result in serious injury or worse. For freer exploration and play, just a little further on are Castle Rocks, which overlook the valley and provide a good excuse to take in the surroundings before descending to the river.

Once down in the valley bottom, the footpath clings to the river's edge for the first ¾ mile. This a particularly beautiful wild stretch where the waterfalls have formed deep pools, some of which would be tempting to sample on a hot day. Along the shallower sections, dipper and grey wagtail can usually be picked out in the summer months, and the heron seems to enjoy fishing here. If the walk was started early in the day, a drink in the beer garden at the Ship Inn a few hundred metres up from the bridge rounds off the outing nicely.

Refreshments Ship Inn at Wincle. Children admitted, beer garden, snacks available.

———————

8. *Ignoring a footbridge and the path that leads to Gradbach, turn left and follow the riverside footpath downstream, which is signposted Danebridge. After a mile, the path climbs away from the riverbank, and a 'New Footpath' leads to a bend in a track by a cottage at Back Dane. Ignore the track. Instead, continue straight on. The footpath leads back to the bridge at the start.*

SHORTER VARIATION
As for 1 to 3 above, then:

i. *Instead of going up the ridge to the right, go straight on along the footpath signposted Gradbach. On reaching a fork in the path on the right of Castle Rocks, take the left fork and continue downhill to the River Dane as for 7 above, then as for 8 above back to the start. (To visit Lud's Church, take the right fork. The entrance is in 200 metres on the right of the footpath.)*

ACCESS BY BUS
To Wincle from Leek (Beresford), Fridays only.

Route 16

(Shorter variation 3 miles)

Hen Cloud, the Roaches and Ramshaw Rocks

Outline   Upper Hulme ~ Hen Cloud ~ The Roaches ~ Well Farm ~ Blue Hills ~ Ramshaw Rocks ~ Naychurch ~ Upper Hulme.

(not recommended for younger children)

Summary   The walk links up three of the most spectacular rock features in the Peak District. Since each stands independent of the other above lower lying ground, the route is a rather up and down affair and seems longer than 5½ miles. The first objective is the summit of Hen Cloud, which has been likened to a miniature Rock of Gilbraltar. From this lofty spot, a descent is made to the gap on the other side of which is the long escarpment of the Roaches. From the gap, a footpath leads around to the foot of the crags, where the remains of an old zoo is situated. An ascent is then made via footsteps and a footpath to the top of the crags. A descent back to the gap follows, from where a combination of tracks, footpaths and a short section of country lane leads up to Ramshaw Rocks. More footpaths and tracks through farmland, muddy in places, are then followed down to Upper Hulme.

Attractions   From the road, Hen Cloud has the look of a mountain peak. This is partly due to its isolation from the rest of the escarpment which forms the Roaches and partly because of the absence of trees below the vertical buttresses guarding its summit. To climb it, a circuitous route to the right is taken which is the least strenuous and the legitimate way up. From the summit, the views of the surrounding countryside are excellent. Looking across at the Roaches, it is possible to make out how it was formed. Successive layers of sand were laid down horizontally millions of years ago when the area was part of a river delta. Under compression, the sand became rock, the composition of the sand determining how hard the rock was. The harder sandstone is known as gritstone. Various forces have since caused these layers to be uplifted to produce such features as the Roaches, Hen Cloud and Ramshaw Rocks as well as the many 'edges' in the Dark Peak.

   An easy descent from Hen Cloud is made to the foot of the Roaches. Nestled beneath the lower tier crags are one or two strange looking artefacts which were part of a zoo that belonged to the Swythamley Estate in the last war. Nearby, stone steps permit an ascent to be made to the foot of a second tier of crags. Facing the top of the steps is a climb which

continued on page 77

73

Route 16

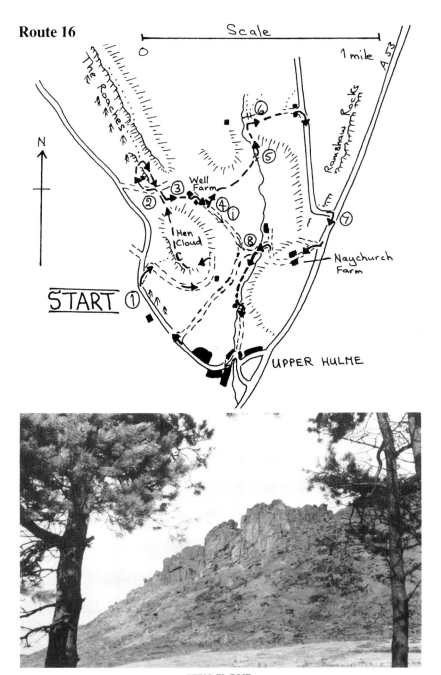

HEN CLOUD

74

Route 16   5½ miles

(Variation 3 miles)

Hen Cloud, the Roaches and Ramshaw Rocks

START   *Due to insufficient parking space in Upper Hulme, the walk is best started ½ mile northwest of the village below the prominent peak-shaped Hen Cloud (G.R. 006614). In respect for the wildlife protected in the Roaches Estate, walkers should keep to the public and concessionary footpaths indicated.*

ROUTE

1. *Take the obvious track that passes directly below the crags of Hen Cloud. Continue along this track beyond the crags and past Roaches House to a footpath on the left. Follow this uphill to the summit of Hen Cloud. From the summit, continue down the other side towards the gap between Hen Cloud and the Roaches. Cross two stiles separated by a narrow strip of field.*

2. *Turn left along a wide footpath. Follow this for a short distance then fork right and continue past a fenced enclosure with an odd-looking building and some strange signs to the foot of the rocks. Steps lead up to the foot of a second tier crag. (From here, the most interesting diversion is to walk left below the crag, then up through an obvious break to the summit. Although it is possible to descend the ridge to the right, the legitimate way is to retrace footsteps back to the footpath going beneath the second tier crags.) Turn right at the top of the steps, and follow the obvious footpath back to the wide footpath in 'the gap'.*

3. *Cross the narrow strip of field again via the two stiles, then go left to Well Farm. Go through a gateway and stay on the left by the grey farm shed. Walk in front of this to reach the track immediately behind the farmhouse. Go along this to a barn on the left. Just past this is a wooden stile on the left.*

4. *Turn left here and follow the wall uphill to a gap on the right at the top of the field. Go through the gap to a stile by a tree. Bear left towards a line of trees and a wall. Continue alongside the wall to a primitive footbridge and stile.*

5. *Cross the stile and turn left to follow the footpath upstream. Continue along this as far as a footbridge directly ahead. Over to the left a farm can be seen. Do not cross the footbridge.*

6. *Turn right and follow the footpath uphill. A track is soon joined which leads to a farm. Go through the farm to a minor road and turn right. Follow the road alongside Ramshaw Rocks to the main road (A.53).*

7. *Turn right and walk along the road for a short distance to a track on the right. Turn right, then fork left over a cattle grid to Naychurch Farm. Go through the farm to a keyhole stile on the right. (Check that the dogs are tethered before doing this!). Bear right down a track after the stile to a very muddy walled track leading down to the stream on the left. Find the driest way to the stile by the stream, cross it and follow the continuation of the disused track to a gravel track.*

8. *Go left over a stile just before the disused track joins the gravel track, and follow the footpath by the stream, then a track down to the ford at Upper Hulme. The pub is up to the left. Otherwise, go across the bridge and continue past the mill for an uphill finish.*

SHORTER VARIATION
As for 1 to 3 above as far as Well Farm, then:

i. *instead of leaving the track as for 4 above, continue along the track to where it bends sharply right. At the same point, a disused track forks left by a wall. Follow the latter for a few metres to a stile in the wall on the right. Continue as for 8 above to Upper Hulme and back to the start.*

ACCESS BY BUS
To Blackshaw Moor only (1 mile south of Upper Hulme) from Leek, Buxton and Sheffield (Potteries), daily.

OVER OWLER TOR   Route 5

finishes up an overhanging crack. This was first climbed by Joe Brown and Don Whillans. Apparently, they tossed a coin for who should have the privilege of going first! The route was aptly named Sloth. Watching climbers hanging about here is a preoccupation of other climbers and is good entertainment for anyone passing by. The footpath to the left from the top of the steps leads to the top of the crag. This diversion is worth it for the better views. And the black grouse, rare to the Peak District, is more likely to be seen flying amongst the rich heather growth on the eastern slopes of the Roaches. It should be noted, however, that the area below the ridge is out of bounds for the sake of the wildlife. From the top of the crag, a footpath leads off the ridge to the right but this, too, is out of bounds, and the proper way back to the gap is by the footpath which passes beneath the second tier.

A pleasant and not uninteresting walk through farmland leads from the gap to Ramshaw Rocks. These crags do not attain the same height as the Roaches or Hen Cloud but their jagged tooth-like appearance is more dramatic than anything on the other two crags. There is also plenty of opportunity for those with sufficient energy left to explore and scramble amongst the rocks, although the youngsters should be adequately supervised in their activities hereabouts.

Upperhulme is essentially a few cottages by an old ford and a former textile mill that is now an engineering works. In other words, the hamlet is more mill than cottages. Nevertheless, it is an interesting little place with a friendly pub that sells good ale. What better way to finish the day's outing!

Refreshments   Ye Olde Rock Inn, Upperhulme. Children admitted, beer garden, snacks available.

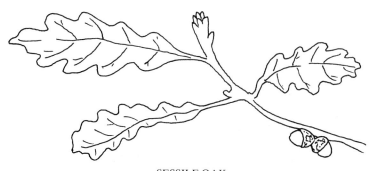

SESSILE OAK

Appendices

ROUTES IN ORDER OF DIFFICULTY

Easier walks - *short (up to 3½ miles)*
Route 5 - *Padley Gorge & Longshaw (Variation II)*
Route 3 - *Birchen Edge and Gardom's Edge*
Route 5 - *Padley Gorge & Longshaw (Variation I)*
Route 7 - *Abney Clough & Bretton (Shorter variation)*
Route 16 - *Hen Cloud & the Roaches*

Medium length (4 to 4½ miles)
Route 2 - *North Chatsworth*
Route 4 - *Froggatt Edge & Derwent Valley (from Grindleford)*
Route 15 - *Lud's Church & Dane Valley (Shorter variation)*
Route 7 - *Abney Clough & Bretton*
Route 14 - *Three Shire Heads*

Long (5 miles or more)
Route 1 - *South Chatsworth & Beeley*
Route 4 - *Froggatt Edge & Derwent Valley (Longer variation)*
Route 5 - *Padley Gorge & Longshaw*
Route 16 - *Hen Cloud, the Roaches & Ramshaw Rocks*

More strenuous walks - *short (up to 3½ miles)*
Route 12 - *White Brow & Middle Moor from Hayfield (Shorter variation)*
Route 10 - *Derwent Edge (Variation I)*
Route 10 - *Derwent Edge (Variation II)*
Route 8 - *Win Hill (Shorter variation)*

Medium length (4 to 4½ miles)
Route 13 - *Windgather Rocks & the Dale of Goyt (Shorter variation)*
Route 12 - *White Brow & Middle Moor from Hayfield*
Route 9 - *Back Tor & Lose Hill (Shorter variation)*

Long (5 miles or more)
Route 13 - *Windgather Rocks & the Dale of Goyt*
Route 15 - *Lud's Church & Dane Valley*
Route 9 - *Back Tor & Lose Hill*
Route 10 - *Derwent Edge*
Route 6 - *Offerton Moor*
Route 8 - *Win Hill*
Route 11 - *Fairbrook Naze & Kinder Edge (and other suggested walks on Kinder)*

BUS OPERATORS TO AND WITHIN THE DARK PEAK (applicable to walks)
Berresford Group .... Tel. Leek 382177
                                                             Stoke 550240
Bower's Coaches .... Tel. Chapel 812204
G. A. Clowes .... Tel. Hartington 433
Crosville Motor Services .... Tel. Chester 315400
                                                             Macclesfield 28855
East Midland Motor Services .... Tel. Chesterfield 75432
Greater Manchester Transport .... Tel. 061-2268181

Potteries Motor Traction Co. .... Tel. Stoke 48811
Silver Service Group .... Tel. Baslow 2246
South Yorkshire Transport .... Tel. Sheffield 755655
Trent Motor Traction Co. .... Tel. Derby 372078

CYCLE HIRE CENTRES

Ashbourne — Mapleton Road. Tel. Ashbourne 43156

Tissington — the building adjacent to the village pond. Tel. Parwich 244

Middleton Top — 4½ miles south of Matlock half way between Middleton and Wirksworth off the B5023, at a picnic site on the High Peak Trail. Tel. Wirksworth 3204

Hartington — 2 the market place. Tel. Hartington 459 or Ashbourne 42629

Parsley Hay - 2 miles south of Monyash and just off the A515 Buxton to Ashbourne, at a picnic site on the High Peak Trail. Tel. Hartington 493

Monsal Head — adjacent to the Monsal Head Hotel on the B6465 1½ miles N.W. of Ashford-in-the-Water. — Tel. Gt. Longstone 505 or Tideswell 871679

Derwent — Fairholmes Picnic Site, below the Derwent Dam, 2 miles north of Ashopton Viaduct (A57-Snake Pass). Tel. 0433-51261

Waterhouses — Waterhouses Station Car Park. Situated near the southern end of the Manifold Track. Tel. 05386-609

Hayfield — Hayfield Station Picnic Site on the Sett Valley Trail, just off the A624 Chapel to Glossop road. Tel. 0663-46222

Lyme Park — Lyme Park National Trust Country Park, Disley. Tel. 06632-2023

Bollington — By the Peak and Plains Discovery Centre, Grimshaw Lane, Bollington, on the Middlewood Way and Cheshire Cycle Way. Tel. 0625-72681

NATURE TRAILS

Black Rocks Trail — ½ mile south of Cromford off the B5036, and starting at the Black Rocks Picnic Area.

Errwood Hall Trail — Goyt Valley. Turn off the A5002 2 miles N.W. of Buxton. The trail starts at a Picnic area.

Ilam Nature Trail — in the grounds of Ilam Hall, Ilam. Tideswell Dale Trail - starts at a Picnic Area 1 mile south of Tideswell.

Padley and Longshaw Nature Trail — starts at Longshaw Lodge, just off the A625 between Sheffield and Hathersage.

Sett Valley Trail — starts at Hayfield Station Picnic site, just off the A624 Chapel to Glossop road.

Lyme Park Nature Trail — Lyme Park, Disley.

COUNTRY PARKS

Alton Towers near Ashbourne. Leisure Park and Gardens, open April to October. Tel. Oakamoor 702458/702449.

Buxton Country Park Woodland walks and interpretation centre. Tel. Buxton 6978.

Chatsworth Farmyard and Adventure Playground. The farm is designed with children in mind, and the adventure playground is superbly constructed. Open Easter to October. Tel. Baslow 2242.

Gulliver's Kingdom, Matlock Bath. Model Village and adventure playground. Open daily. Tel. Matlock 55970.

Riber Castle Wildlife Park near Matlock. British and European birds and animals, vintage car and motorcycle collection, children's playground and model railway. Tel. Matlock 2073.

Lyme Park National Trust Country Park, Disley. A deer park centred on Lyme Hall, with adventure playground.

RAINY DAY ALTERNATIVES
MUSEUMS, HOUSES AND INDUSTRIAL ARCHAEOLOGY

Aquarium and Waxworks Museum, Matlock Bath. Tel. Matlock 3624.

Buxton Micrarium. Nature seen through microscopes. Open April to November. Tel. Buxton 78662.

Buxton Museum. Archaeological relics of the Peak District. Closed on Mondays. Tel. Buxton 4658.

Caudwell's Mill, Rowsley. A working, water-power, roller flour mill. Open Easter to October. Tel. Matlock 734374.

Cavendish House Museum, Castleton. Houses the Ollernshaw Collection of Blue John, etc. Open daily all year. Tel. Hope Valley 20642.

Chatsworth House. Home of the Duke of Devonshire, open April to October. Tel. Baslow 2242.

Crich Tramway Museum. Turn off A6 at Whatstandwell or off A610 at Bullbridge. Tram rides, period street etc. Open April to October. Tel. Ambergate 2565.

Cromford Canal Wharf. Canal trips by horse-drawn boat. Tel. Wirksworth 3921.

Cromford Mill. Arkwright's waterpowered cotton spinning mill. Open all year. Tel. Wirksworth 4297.

Dinting Railway Centre, Glossop. Collection of steam locomotives. Open daily. Tel. Glossop 5596.

Haddon Hall, near Bakewell. The Duke of Rutland's Medieval Hall. Open Tuesdays to Saturdays, April to September. Tel. Bakewell 2855.

Longnor Folk Museum. Exhibits and spinning demonstrations. Open Saturdays and Bank Holidays from Spring Bank Holiday week-end to end of first week in September, 2.30 - 4.30.

Longshaw Estate, Foxhouse, next to A625 Sheffield-Hathersage road. Described in Route 5. Shop, cafe and Information Centre on the site.

Magpie Mine, Sheldon. Remains of lead mine including chimneys, engine house and winding gear. Information about access from Peak District Mining Museum, Matlock Bath. Tel. Matlock 3834.

Middleton Top Engine House. Winding engine of former Cromford and High Peak Railway. Open Sundays and first Saturday of each month, when the engine is in steam. Tel. Wirksworth 3204.

Old House Museum, Bakewell. Tudor house and Folk Museum. Open daily, Easter to October. Tel. Bakewell 3647.

Peak District Mining Museum, Matlock Bath. Exhibits and displays illustrating 2000 years of lead mining. Climbing shaft between floors for children. Open daily all year. Tel. Matlock 3834.

Peak Rail, Buxton. Steam rides, April to September at week-ends and Bank Holidays. Tel. Buxton 77763.

Peveril Castle, Castleton. Impressive ruined Norman castle with keep. Splendid views over Castleton and surrounding countryside. Open daily all year. Tel. Hope Valley 20613.

SWIMMING POOLS

There are indoor pools at Ashbourne, Buxton, Leek and Matlock.

All the information given here was correct on publication, but times of opening etc. are sometimes altered at short notice, so do please check before setting off on a grand expedition!

PUBS AND INNS CATERING FOR FAMILIES

Below is a list of some of the village pubs and inns in the area covered by this guide, the licensees of which make provision for families with young children. To locate them, refer to the map at the beginning of the guide.

Beeley — Devonshire Arms.

Castleton — Bull's Head Hotel and Castle Hotel.

Edale — Old Nag's Head.

Fernilee — 2½ miles south of Whaley Bridge on A5002. Shady Oak.

Flash — New Inn.

Foxhouse — Fox House Inn. On the A625, Sheffield to Hathersage road.

Grindleford — Sir William Inn.

Grouse Inn — 2½ miles north of Calver on B6054.

Hathersage — George Hotel, Hathersage Inn, Scotchman's Pack, Little John.

Hayfield — Packhorse Inn.

Hope — Cheshire Cheese Inn and Woodroffe Arms.

Ladybower — Ladybower Inn.

Leadmill — ½ mile south of Hathersage on B6001 to Grindleford. Plough Inn.

Little Hayfield — 1 mile north of Hayfield on A624, Chapel to Glossop road. Lantern Pike.

Robin Hood — 1¾ miles east of Baslow on A619 to Chesterfield. Robin Hood Inn.

Snake Inn — On A57, Snake Pass.

Upper Hulme — On the A53 Leek to Buxton road, near the Roaches, Ye Olde Rock Inn.

Wincle — South of the A54 Congleton ot Buxton road. Ship Inn.

Family Walks Series

Family Walks in the White Peak. Norman Taylor. 1985. Reprinted 1985. Revised 1987. ISBN 0 907758 09 6. £2.70.
> Judged by The Great Outdoors to be "the best Peak District short walks guide yet published."

Family Walks in the Dark Peak. Norman Taylor. 1986. Revised 1988. ISBN 0 907758 16 9. £2.70.
> Companion to the first title in the Series.

Family Walks in the Cotswolds. Gordon Ottewell. 1986. Revised 1988. ISBN 0 907758 15 0. £2.70.
> Covers an area between Gloucester and Stow-on-the-Wold.

Family Walks around Bristol, Bath and the Mendips. Nigel Vile. 1987. ISBN 09907759 19 3. £2.70.

Family Walks in Hereford and Worcester. Gordon Ottewell. 1988. ISBN 0 907758 20 7. £2.85.

Family Walks in the Downs and Vales of Wiltshire. Nigel Vile. 1988. ISBN 0 907758 21 5. £2.85.

Ready Spring 1989.

Family Walks in South Yorkshire. Norman Taylor. £3.00. ISBN 0907758 25 8.
Family Walks in the Wye Valley. Heather and Jon Hurley. £3.00. From Hay-on-Wye to Chepstow. ISBN 0 907758 26 6.
Family Walks in Mid-Wales. Laurence Main. £3.00. Between Snowodnia and the Brecon Beacons. ISBN 0 907758 27 4.

In preparation:
Family Walks in Gwent
Family Walks in Shropshire
Family Walks around Newbury
Family Walks in South Gloucestershire
Family Walks in North Staffordshire
Family Walks in Cheshire

Scarthin Books of Cromford are the leading Peak District specialists in secondhand and antiquarian books, and are always ready to purchase large or small collections of good books and music, ancient or modern.
Contact: Dr. D. J. Mitchell by letter, or phone Wirksworth 3272.
